THE GREAT PLAINS

READING
FOR YOUNG PEOPLE

THE GREAT
PLAINS

MILDRED LAUGHLIN

AMERICAN LIBRARY ASSOCIATION

Chicago 1979

READING FOR YOUNG PEOPLE

A series of annotated bibliographies of fiction and nonfiction titles, compiled for readers from the primary grades through the tenth grade and designed to focus on the history and character of each region of these United States.

THE MIDWEST by *Dorothy Hinman and Ruth Zimmerman*

Edited by *F. Laverne Carroll,* The University of Oklahoma, Norman

THE GREAT PLAINS by *Mildred Laughlin*

Library of Congress Cataloging in Publication Data

Laughlin, Mildred.
    Reading for young people.

    Includes index.
    1. Great Plains—Juvenile literature—Bibliography.
I. Title. II. Title: The Great Plains.
Z1251.W5L38 [F591]   016.978   78-27242
ISBN 0-8389-0265-0

Printed in the United States of America

CONTENTS

ACKNOWLEDGMENTS

Preparation of this publication necessitated hundreds of hours of work in order to select and annotate the literary works that best represent a specific state within the Great Plains region. In addition, wise selection required familiarity with the state which comes only from residence within its borders.

These faithful state committee members made this work a reality through their efforts: for Kansas, Helen White, School Library Consultant, Wichita Public Schools; for Nebraska, Nancy Chu, Southeast Nebraska Network Librarian, Nebraska Library Commission; for North Dakota, Ruth C. McMartin, Director of Instructional Resources, Fargo Public Schools; and for South Dakota, Edith B. Siegrist, Assistant Professor, University of South Dakota, Library Media Division.

Dr. Frances Laverne Carroll, Series Editor and Professor of Library Science at the University of Oklahoma, and Herbert Bloom, Senior Editor, American Library Association, contributed to the planning of the series and assisted in the preparation of the manuscript.

Professor Frederick Wezeman, Director of The University of Iowa School of Library Science, was generous in his support and encouragement during the conduct of the project. Especial gratitude must be expressed to my colleague, Barbara Poston, and my editor, Sylvia Royt, for the countless hours spent in assisting with editing and indexing, and to Pat Kondora for her expert typing and pleasant attitude toward the corrections necessitated by unavoidable inconsistencies resulting from commitee endeavors.

Mildred Laughlin
Associate Professor
School of Library Science
The University of Iowa

INTRODUCTION

Many state departments of public instruction either have requirements that state history be taught in the public schools or that elements of state history be included in the K–12 social studies program. Often, if the latter approach is used, a regional blend of history and geography becomes the content base.

Current teaching techniques demand a multiplicity of materials, and curriculum consultants or committees have answered that need by preparing bibliographies of available titles, often all-inclusive, leaving any judgment about literary quality to the user. If listings are appended to units of work, they frequently contain only factual materials and ignore the well-done fiction that presents an accurate portrayal of scenes and conditions characteristic of the area. Thus, the purpose of the Great Plains bibliography is three-fold:

1. To introduce the young people living in the Great Plains region to books dealing with their cultural heritage
2. To help young people of other regions of the United States understand the cultural and social influences that shaped the lives of Great Plains dwellers
3. To serve as a selection tool for librarians, teachers, and students as they plan units of work or special projects in which the cultural heritage of the Great Plains is identified.

The selection of states to include in the Great Plains bibliography was arbitrary, as there are no discrete geographical-political divisions which all authorities designate as the Great Plains. Parts of Oklahoma and Texas are sometimes included, along with Kansas, Nebraska, North Dakota, South Dakota, and the eastern areas of Montana and Wyoming.

1

However, in a bibliography primarily concerned with the social and cultural heritage of the Great Plains as evidenced in its literary works, the states of Texas and Oklahoma are more appropriately associated with the Southwest, while Montana and Wyoming are regarded primarily as Rocky Mountain states. Therefore, the states of Kansas, Nebraska, North Dakota, and South Dakota were selected as the focus of this bibliography. Their commonality is very apparent.

The terrain of each state follows a similar geographic pattern, mostly flat land sloping from a lower eastern border to a higher elevation in the west. Many of the pioneers who followed the Santa Fe and Oregon Trails remained on the Great Plains instead of continuing the long trek to California or Oregon. Among these settlers were immigrants from several European countries, bringing with them their own traditions, foods, and music. Thus, the art and folklore of diverse peoples form the cultural heritage of the region. These include the Plains Indians who, driven from their lands and decimated by wars with the settlers and by their diseases, were forced to settle on reservations. Yet we seek to evoke their culture by means of the towns and rivers that bear their names, the crafts that many now seek to learn and emulate, and the ceremonial dances that are featured in the region's celebrations.

Summer rodeos recall the cowboy whose cattle grazed the prairie grass on the open range. Museums and restored villages preserve the pioneer past, mute evidence of the courageous spirit which withstood the harsh climate of the Great Plains to establish the agricultural economy that characterizes the region and continues to influence the social life and customs of the people. Heroes of fact and fiction, personified by such men as Buffalo Bill Cody and Wyatt Earp, also left a legendary heritage that symbolizes the enchantment of the plains, an enchantment that should not be lost to young people.

The primary emphasis for the total bibliography was on creative literature—fiction, biography, folklore, poetry, drama, music—although general information books in such areas as social science, geography, and science were not excluded. Selection criteria included literary quality, regional application, and appropriateness for a specific grade level. It is unfortunate that few primary-level books were available for inclusion. However, concern for this fact was lessened by the knowledge that curriculum emphasis demanding materials about the Great Plains usually occurs at an upper elementary or secondary level.

Books presenting all aspects of the Great Plains significant to appreciation of the region's cultural heritage were not available; thus some marginal books were annotated. The decision to include out-of-print titles (identified by the symbol "op") also related to availability. If a valuable approach was not evidenced in another work and there were many copies still held in library collections, the out-of-print book was included. By this means the value of a particular title could be noted, its use increased, and its unwarranted discarding avoided. In addition, when a paperback or other reprint edition of an out-of-print book was known to be available, this information was included in the citation. Note that the symbol "op" usually refers to the original edition of an out-of-print title.

Each entry includes complete bibliographical data and a brief quote from the book to identify style, theme, strong characterization, or mood, followed by an original annotation. The brief descriptive annotation indicates the book's content, scope, and regional value. The selection of works to include and the preparation of the annotations were assigned to a chairperson from each state who sought the advice of other professionals to determine the merits and limitations of each book. A suggested general grade range—Primary (P), Intermediate (I), Junior high (J), and Senior high (S)—was included to aid the user in finding materials appropriate for a specific level.

The annotated bibliography is not all-inclusive but represents each state chairperson's efforts to select a maximum of 100 books with regional value. The arrangement of the bibliography is alphabetical by author within the designated areas of Fiction; Folktales; Poetry, Drama, and Music; Biography and Personal Accounts; and Other Informational Books. Illustrators other than the author of the work are noted in the bibliographic citation, when appropriate. The unconventional decision to place biographies in alphabetical order by author was made in an attempt to provide easier access to the books whose titles did not reveal the subject and whose authors were often better known nationally than the local personages who provided the basis for the work. Paperback editions are indicated; if the publisher is the same as for the hardcover edition, only a date is given. The series title, if appropriate, is included also.

A list of state books submitted by each chairperson, alphabetically arranged by author within the broadly designated subject areas of the main bibliography, one for each of the four Great Plains states, is also included. The number preceding each entry in these lists refers to the entry in the annotated bibliography. Several titles may appear on more than one list, and a few of general value, which were added by the editor, are not included in any of the state lists.

Further access to the bibliography is provided through a simple author, title, and subject index. Although not always all-inclusive in nature, it represents the best efforts of four chairpersons who could not always anticipate whether a local subject would represent a unique curriculum emphasis within the entire region. The general criterion for inclusion of nonfiction works in the index was three or more pages dealing with the identified subject, and specific pagination is indicated.

For the convenience of the users of the bibliography, the addresses of regional publishers or suppliers of particular local importance not found in *Books in Print* are given in the Directory of Regional Publishers . . . following the State Lists. If some out-of-print books are still available within the state, that source is also noted.

Nonbook materials are not included in the annotated bibliography. As yet, creative audiovisual works relating to a specific state or region are limited, if they exist at all. Their value is primarily local rather than regional and thus seemed inappropriate.

ANNOTATED BIBLIOGRAPHY

FICTION

1   Aldrich, Bess Streeter. *Journey into Christmas and*   (J, S)
    Other Stories. Illus. by James Aldrich. Appleton,   op
    1928. 265p.

> How could a little sod house know such enchantment?

Family and neighbors sharing together provides the theme for this collection of stories about Christmas in Nebraska. In the title story Margaret Staley is able to surround herself with those she loves through memories, even though she is alone on Christmas Eve for the first time in her life. Old Jed Miller in "Another Brought Gifts" saved his quarters to share with the children on Christmas Eve and ultimately gave his life to save theirs. A selection from *A Lantern in Her Hand* entitled "Christmas on the Prairie" recalls the year 1874 when grasshoppers destroyed the crops and only the coming of the barrel from home gave Abbie the courage to begin planning for Christmas. The collection ends with remembrances from the author's own childhood.

2   Aldrich, Bess Streeter, *A Lantern in Her Hand.*   (J, S)
    Appleton, 1928. 307p. (Paperback ed., Grosset, nd)   op

> When Will took the long drive to Nebraska City for supplies, her desolation seemed complete.

In Abbie Deal's life the reader sees the strength and determination of the pioneer woman. Despite crop failures, grasshoppers, sickness, and the death of her husband, she reared and educated their five children. Her death alone seemed a fitting close to a courageous life.

3   Aldrich, Bess Streeter.   *The Rim of the Prairie.*   (S)
     Appleton, 1925.   352p.   (Paperback ed., Univ. of   op
     Nebraska Pr., 1966)

   For here, as everywhere, drama ebbs and flows like the billowing
   of the seas of yellow wheat.

Nancy Moore had lived in Maple City, Nebraska, with Uncle Jud
and Aunt Biny for eighteen years before suddenly going East. Her
return set off a chain of events involving the writer Warner Field, the
banker's daughter, and the "Bee House" boarders. The mystery of
Nancy's birth, solved after a tornado threatens the countryside, adds
appeal to this sensitive portrayal both of small-town life and of the
strength of the early pioneers. Despite two racial slurs not considered
unacceptable fifty years ago, the story has merit; and readers may
enjoy comparing it with Thornton Wilder's *Our Town.*

4   Annixter, Jane and Paul.   *Buffalo Chief.*   Holiday,   (I, J)
     1958.   219p.

   The great herd, already dwindled, will shrink rapidly until it is a
   great herd no longer! The buffalo is our totem. As they go, we go.

The stories of Kahtanka, a great buffalo bull, as he strove for the
survival of his herd, and of Hawk, a great Sioux warrior, as he fought
for the survival of his people, are paralleled in this story. Sympathetic
treatment of Sioux life and customs at the time of Sitting Bull is given
through the eyes of Standing Elk, a shaman, the tribal oracle of the
Oglalas.

5   Barker, Mary Libal.   *Milenka's Happy Summer.*   (I)
     Illus. by Paul Lantz.   Dodd, 1961.   187p.   op

   "Dedechek will stay the whole summer." Mama's brown eyes
   twinkled and she looked like a happy little girl.

A visit from Milenka's Grandfather Valek, called Dedechek by
his grandchildren, was always a special event. He would stay all summer, allowing time for long walks, fishing trips, and stories of his life
in the old country, Czechoslovakia. The days pass peacefully and
happily in this story of Nebraska at the turn of the century. Lovers of
pioneer stories will be delighted with the details of sauerkraut making,
goose plucking, and kolache baking in this pleasing account of a national group whose settlement in Nebraska has influenced many aspects
of local culture.

6   Benchley, Nathaniel.   *Only Earth and Sky Last*   (J)
     Forever.   Harper, 1972.   189p.   (Paperback ed., 1972)

   I thought of my plan to do great deeds to impress Lashuka's grandmother, and it became clearer than ever that this agency was not the place to do them.

A young Indian boy, Dark Elk, must prove to his tribe and to himself that he has courage to fight for freedom, primarily to be worthy in the eyes of the grandmother of his true love. Fate conspires against him throughout the story and he seems destined to be a loser. The finale of the story is his version of the Battle of the Little Big Horn in which he loses Lashuka forever. As Dark Elk relates his tragic story, the reader feels sympathy for all the red men who were unfairly treated by the "Blue Coats" and the whites.

7   Bliss, Ronald G.   *Indian Softball Summer or Kickapoos*   (I)
     Never Say Good-bye.   Illus. by William Moyer.
     Dodd, 1974.   127p.

     "Why do you play softball?" asked Rand after awhile. "Baseball's a better game."

When Rand Cogburn, a baseball buff from New York, visits his cousin Clyde in western Kansas for the summer, he doesn't think much of the game of softball. That is, he doesn't until he plays with the Ludell Leapers. He soon finds there is more to the game than he thought and more to the players, too. Among the unique features of the Ludell Leapers are a catcher named Dirty Mutt, an Indian short-stop who has never played the game before, and the absence of an adult manager. Rand has a summer of adventure and is much surprised when the Indian shortstop turns out to be a girl.

8   Bonham, Barbara.   *Challenge of the Prairie.*   (I, J)
     Bobbs-Merrill, 1965.   150p.

     I decided last night we'd stay here instead of going back. . . . That means we've got a lot of work to do.

The unexpected death of Toby's father a year before their home-stead claim becomes final leaves the family with a difficult problem. Shall they remain in Nebraska or return East? The decision rests with the eldest son Toby, who will be expected to assume most of the family responsibility. They remain on the claim and face the challenges of a grasshopper plague, drought, squatters, and Toby's own inexperi-ence. This account of life in Nebraska just after the Civil War makes vivid reading for those who prefer a fictional treatment of history.

9   Bothwell, Jean.   *Peter Holt, P.K.*   Illus. by   (I)
     Margaret Ayer.   Harcourt, 1950.   214p.   op

     Peter was used to being called a P.K. . . . Having a minister for a father had always seemed a proud thing.

Being a minister's son in a new town carried with it a unique set of problems for Peter. Making friends and showing them that being a P.K. did not make you different was sometimes difficult. However, Peter and Molly, his twin, enjoy the small midwestern town of Millersville and soon adjust to their surroundings. The author used Madison, Nebraska, as a model for Millersville and creates a well-drawn picture of small-town life and a believable set of characters. Peter's handling of typical fifth-grade problems makes an entertaining, light story. *The Red Barn Club* (Harcourt, 1954) continues the story of the Holt family in Millersville.

10   Bothwell, Jean.   *Tree House at Seven Oaks: A Story*   (J)
      of the Flat Water Country in 1853.   Illus. by Bob   op
      Hodgell.   Abelard-Schuman, 1957.   239p.

    I must start west. When I go I'd like to take Thad with me. . . . I need him with me.

When Thad accompanies his father, Major Curtin, to the Nebraska-Kansas Territory, the boy's dreams of adventure come true. After childhood years spent in Washington, D.C., the Missouri River trading post at Sarpy's Landing was a welcome change. The unrest of unhappy Indians, disturbed by the encroachment of white settlers into their hunting grounds, and pending legislation to open the land for settlement add excitement to Thad's new life in the Nebraska of 1853. The story lends new dimensions to the lives of such actual historical figures as Peter Sarpy and Joseph La Flesche.

11   Breneman, Mary Worthy.   *The Land They Possessed.*   (S)
      Macmillan, 1956.   335p.   op

    This is the frontier. The land is free for those who'll live on it and work it.

In the 1880s thousands of German-Russians emigrated to the midwestern states to escape conscription and taxation in the Ukraine. Some came to the Ipswich area of South Dakota where they conquered the prairie and, in the melting-pot tradition, became Americans. The newcomers are seen here through the eyes of the Wards, who also have a tree claim. Their daughter Michal overcomes the nationality-consciousness of her English parents to marry Karl Gross, handsome son of a "Rooshan" family. Some historical inaccuracies, such as Sitting Bull being killed at Wounded Knee, do not detract markedly from the story.

12   Brown, Marion Marsh.   *Frontier Beacon.*   (J)
      Westminster, 1953.   187p.   op

    Never lose sight of your dream, Son, no matter what happens.

When his father moved the family from a slave state, Missouri, to a free Nebraska territory, Jud Stuart's hopes for the future were dashed. The harsh realities of surviving and developing a farm made his dreams of a printing office seem irrelevant, especially since a newspaperman needed an education. This goal seemed even less attainable after the death of his father required that Jud manage the farm. Yet each time that goal seemed to slip beyond his grasp, Jud found a way to recapture it. Set in the years just prior to the Civil War, the story captures the excitement of the times, includes a strong romantic element, and presents the young Nebraska territory in relation to a nation approaching disaster.

13   Brown, Marion Marsh. *Marnie.* Westminster,   (J)
      1971.   189p.   op
        I wonder if everything's that way, if no matter how nice things are, after a while you want a change.

A Nebraska farm in the early twentieth century provides a perfect place for Marnie to view change as it occurs—in seasons, her friends, and herself. Her romantic and imaginative mind finds plenty of ideas to ponder and conclusions to pursue. While caught in the routine of farm life, she faces conflicts between her lingering childhood and emerging maturity, prompting her to question her own feelings and reactions. Young readers will identify with Marnie while gaining an accurate picture of rural Nebraska in an earlier era.

14   Brown, Marion Marsh. *Prairie Teacher.* Avalon   (J, S)
      Books, 1957.   223p.   op
        We respect our teachers in Valley Junction.

Trudy Martin's first teaching assignment in Valley Junction, Nebraska, was an unattractive alternative to the career in television she had envisioned for herself. However, her plans were postponed when a bout with polio left her with a limp. Although she experiences all the traumas common to young, inexperienced teachers, she makes two completely unanticipated discoveries. She finds she enjoys teaching and she loves Valley Junction, sandstorms and all. Set in the sandhill country of the western part of the state, this book gives a representative picture of the educational process in a small Nebraska town in the 1950s.

15   Calhoun, Mary. *High Wind for Kansas.* Illus. by   (P, I)
      W. T. Mars.   Morrow, 1965.   45p.   op
        Why that western wind will peel off a section of the prairie—creek bed, cottonwoods, and all—and sail it away.

Windwagon Thomas tried to harness the wind to propel wagons across the prairies, and the true story of his efforts is the basis for this

9

expanded tall tale. Jones, the hero of Calhoun's story, was to sail his windwagon to Council Grove. If the idea worked, a new mode of prairie transportation could be developed. Everything went well until the wagon set out on its own course. This funny anecdote is just right for telling and may inspire research about the actual event. Line drawings add to the book's appeal.

16   Carlson, Natalie Savage. *The Tomahawk Family.*   (P, I)
Illus. by Stephen Cook.   Harper, 1960.   170p.

> Why do you always act Indian, Grandma? . . . Why don't you talk good English like me and Frankie?

Orphaned Alice and Frank Tomahawk begin a new school year on a Sioux reservation in South Dakota. The logs in their cabin corners were like clasped fingers holding the family tightly together. However conflicts between the old ways and the new emerge. Frank longs to be a brave warrior, Alice wants to become "a good American," and Grandma has no interest in either schools or education. This book is useful for dealing with adjustment problems for any children.

17   Cather, Willa. *My Ántonia.* Illus. by W. T. Benda.   (J, S)
Houghton, 1918.   371p.   (Paperback ed., 1961)

> And I guess everybody thinks about old times, even the happiest people.

In Jim Burden's memories of his friendship with Antonia Shimerdas, the frustrations of life on a pioneer Nebraska farm are revealed. The Bohemian Shimerdas family spoke no English, and the first winter in a cave "no better than a badger hole" was full of privation for them. Antonia suffered from the suicide of her father, the ugly nature of her brother Ambrosch, the prejudice of a small town against the immigrant hired girls, and the back-breaking toil in the fields; yet she did not despair. Her love for the farm, her husband, and her children exemplifies the indomitable spirit of the pioneer woman.

18   Cather, Willa. *O Pioneers!* Houghton, 1913.   309p.   (S)
(Paperback ed., 1962).

> We come and go, but the land is always here.

Alexandra Bergson had the strength and vision of her pioneer father and was willing to mortgage the family farm to buy up surrounding acres. Hard work paid off, but after sixteen years, Alexandra was alone with only the hopes of a college education for her younger brother and the memories of an early friendship. Tragedy mars her life, but in the end she is able to find hope and strength in the return of one she loves. The book presents an excellent saga of life on the Nebraska prairie.

19   Cather, Willa.   *Obscure Destinies.*   Knopf, 1932.   (S)
          229p.   (Paperback ed., Random, 1974)

> They didn't often exchange opinions, even in Czech,—it was as if they thought the same thought together.

Three stories comprise this collection which presents rural and smalltown life in the West. "Neighbor Rosicky" heads the gallant Czech family which faces crop failure and hard times in Nebraska, yet continues to enjoy life. "Old Mrs. Harris" came from Tennessee with her family and is strangely satisfied with the family role which townspeople deem little better than that of a slave. "Two Friends" in Kansas let Bryan's nomination come between them, and their pride resisted a reconciliation. The reader senses the waste of lost friendship, resulting in an unhappy destiny very unlike the deaths which end the other two tales.

20   Chandler, Edna Walker.   *Chaff in the Wind.*   Pageant,   (S)
          1964.   389p.   (Paperback ed., Sierra Printing, 1977)   op

> He had cast his lot with the wheat country. The wheat country had rewarded him richly.

During the time of the great agricultural and industrial expansion, John Halegren and his family, immigrants first from Sweden and then from the tenements of New York, engage in the struggle of survival against the forces of nature. All characters are bound to the wheat whether they are drawn to it, as John is, or run from it, as Rachel does. Courage, despair, rejection, and love for each other, for the land, and for the wheat are key elements in this story.

21   Cleaver, Vera and Bill.   *Dust of the Earth.*   (J)
          Lippincott, 1975.   159p.   (Paperback ed., New
          American Library, 1977)

> I am hard put to it to describe the Badlands of South Dakota, their many-colored soils, their spirit shapes. . . . They bring to my mind a picture of an old, lost, royal city I have never seen.

When Grandfather Bacon willed them his farm near Chokecherry in the Badlands, fourteen-year-old Fern Drawn's family moved to the first home they had ever owned. The family, seen through adolescent eyes, triumphed over such adversities as drought, blizzards, and lambing time, growing toward togetherness.

22   Coatsworth, Elizabeth.   *The Sod House.*   Macmillan,   (P, I)
          1967.   64p.

> This is Kansas. . . . Oh how many flowers there are and so many meadowlarks singing! I love it! I love it!

Seeking freedom in the New World, the Trauble family left Germany and settled first in Massachusetts and then on a farm near Osawatomie in Kansas Territory. Concerned over the slavery question, Friedrich Trauble urged the admittance of Kansas to the Union as a free state. This political involvement embroiled the family in a variety of dangers. The bravery of seven-year-old Ilse was displayed as she rescued the cow from a prairie fire set to drive out the Trauble family.

23 Constant, Alberta Wilson. *Those Miller Girls.*   (I, J)
    Illus. by Joe and Beth Krush. Crowell, 1965. 303p.

  Rule Number One. . . . The Family Sticks Together, No Matter What.

After much coaxing from his two motherless daughters, Professor Miller purchased a bright red, horseless Great Smith in Topeka, and the family traveled to their new home in Gloriosa. The car became the center for a number of adventures as the fun-loving girls adjusted to the new life. Line drawings enhance the text. This book and its sequel, *The Motoring Millers* (Crowell, 1969), are excellent for reading aloud.

24 Coon, Martha Sutherland. *Georgie's Capital.* Illus.   (I)
    by Corinne Keyser. Harvey House, 1967. 205p.

  Georgie burst past him into the sitting room and screamed, "Wake up, Linnie! Papa is elected, and Pierre is the capital. Linnie, wake up! We won!"

Based on remembrances of her own girlhood in Pierre, Mrs. Coon tells how the town became the capital of the new state of South Dakota in 1890. Georgia Clark, a "nine-going-on-ten-year-old-girl," and her friend, Susan Hamilton, play with dolls, celebrate Memorial Day and the Fourth of July, and even ride on a mule-drawn streetcar; but their most exciting adventure is being "secretaries" for the Pierre-for-Capital Committee. Chapter 18 is a glossary of "Expressions Used in Georgie's Day," including terms such as baseburner, bustle, and carpet beater.

25 Dahl, Borghild. *Karen.* Dutton, 1947. 313p.   (J)
                                                                        op

  "We're not going back," Karen said. . . . "The land is good. . . . We can always get a house and other buildings. That only takes time and hard work."

Having emigrated from Norway in the 1870s, Karen Elvaas combined hard work with courage and determination, first as a servant girl in Dubuque, Iowa, and then as Arne Forsdale's bride in Dakota Territory. The optimism she exhibited in the face of seemingly unsurmountable obstacles exemplifies the story of many Dakota pioneer women.

26 Dahl, Borghild. *This Precious Year.* Dutton, 1964. (J)
159p. op

> Even indoors she could feel the grit under her feet, and outdoors it was everywhere—she breathed it, tasted it, felt it in her eyes and nose and ears.

The author drew from her experiences as a teacher at South Dakota's Augustana College in the 1930s for this month-by-month account of Helia Singstad's senior year at Nidaros College. Despite the drought and depression, the year was made precious by the sacrifices of her family and the friendship of Peter Leegaard. A three-day rain which revived their desolate Dakota farm, Helia's graduation, and her acceptance of a teaching position at Three Oaks promise a brighter future.

27 Davis, Clyde Brion. *Nebraska Coast.* Illus. by (S)
Edward Shenton. Farrar, 1939. 423p. op

> "We're going to get away from this narrow-minded, war-crazy community."

The Macdougall family had been labeled "Copperheads," not because they sympathized with the South but because they were against war. When a letter arrives from a cousin in Nebraska territory describing the rich, open land, Jack Macdougall's family leaves New York to seek this unknown, enticing place. Fictional characters are interwoven with actual people and events, depicting life on the Nebraska prairie. The explicit language of the characters, as well as the attitudes toward Indians and other minority groups characteristic of many people of that era, make this selection one which may be selected for older readers who will view the work within its historical perspective.

28 DeLeeuw, Adele Louise. *Blue Ribbons for Meg.* (I)
Illus. by Mac Schweitzer. Little, 1950. 145p. op
(Paperback ed., Scholastic, 1958)

> She hadn't known that there would be so many things to get used to, that she would miss her parents and her friends so much.

Captain Armstrong's children thought having a cousin from Boston come to live with them for a year would be wonderful. However, when nine-year-old Meg arrived at their U.S. Cavalry outpost at Fort Miles (a fictional Fort Meade) on the eastern edge of the Black Hills, they found her too easily frightened by Indians, prairies, and coyotes, and too much a lady who read books and knitted. A pinto pony, Papoose, and a puppy of her own named Pinto transformed Meg's year into a happy one.

29   DeRegniers, Beatrice Schenk. *The Snow Party.*   (P)
      Illus. by Reiner Zimmik.   Pantheon, 1959. unp.

   The old woman said, "I'm mighty lonely here with just you and
the chickens for company. I'd like to give me a party and have plenty
of folks in."

A little old man and a little old woman who lived on a Dakota
farm were lonely until the big blizzard came. Many adults, children,
babies, dogs, and other pets sought refuge in the little old farmhouse;
and the arrival of the KM Bakery man contributed to the party atmosphere. The light treatment of the blizzard, a prairie hazard, is fun
reading.

30   Dick, Trella Lamson. *Tornado Jones.* Illus. by Mary   (I)
      Stevens.   Follett, 1953.   286p.   op

   Good overbalances bad. At last he was like "other folks" with ancestors to talk about.

Tornado Jones could not believe grandma's positive attitude as
they faced the dismal fate of living with stingy Uncle Bill and Aunt Min
when their small Nebraska home was flooded to make way for the dam.
In addition, Tornado's family background and name both were a mystery he wanted to solve. Paul Travis, whose father was a dam engineer,
became Tornado's first real friend of his own age. The two boys solved
the mysteries of his heritage and of the two men who seemed to be digging for buried gold in the canyon. Grandma's faith triumphed in this
simple, appealing story of the people and lifestyle in a small Nebraska
sandhill community.

31   Erdman, Loula Grace. *Many a Voyage.* Centennial   (S)
      ed.   Dodd, 1967.   309p.   op

   I have taken an oath to do impartial justice according to the dictates
of my judgment and for the highest good of the country.

Senator Edmund Ross of Kansas cast the deciding vote that saved
President Andrew Johnson from conviction during the impeachment
trial in 1868. Ross had been expected to vote for impeachment and in-
curred the wrath of his fellow senators and his constituents when he
did not. The novel, written from the viewpoint of Ross's wife, Fannie,
explores the making of this remarkable man and the devotion, trust, and
adaptability of his family.

32   Fernald, Helen Clark. *Plow the Dew Under.*   (J, S)
      Longmans, 1952.   301p.   op

   How quickly the dead prairie came alive under the hands of the
new settlers!

Nicolas Plaevsky and his fellow Mennonites came from the Crimea to Kansas in 1874, seeking freedom and a suitable place to raise their winter wheat. Severe winters, locusts, and prairie fires plagued them, but perseverence led to the establishment of a farming community which was to make an outstanding contribution to the state.

33 Field, Elsie Kimmell. *Prairie Winter*. Illus. by (P)
Bernard Case. Lothrop, 1959. 160p. op

The brakeman helped them off one by one down the steep steps, and they stood in Dakota.

Papa was the engineer on a train in Iowa; but when he won the right to homestead on Standing Rock Indian Reservation, he moved Mama, Elsie, and John to their government claim near McIntosh, South Dakota. The problems of homesteading are evidenced in authentic details of such events as building the house and digging the well. Descriptions of the buffalo grass, the folding bed, and the big, round heating stove bring the period into focus.

34 Fisher, Aileen. *Homestead of the Free*. Illus. by (I, J)
Peter Burchard. (American Heritage) Aladdin, op
1953. 192p.

Kansas must be saved for freedom.

The Morse family moved to Lawrence in Kansas Territory in 1855. Mr. Morse, an attorney, became involved in the political struggles of the Free Staters. The dangers to life and property are vividly portrayed, and the family story thus brings alive the historic era of Kansas history termed "Bleeding Kansas."

35 Garland, Hamlin. *Main-Travelled Roads*. Harper, (S)
1909. 377p. (Paperback ed., Signet Classics, 1962;
Brown Bk. Co., nd)

A record of the privations and hardships of the men and women who subdued the midland wilderness.

This collection of short stories was based on Garland's experiences in South Dakota and dedicated to his parents "whose half-century pilgrimage on the main-travelled road of life has brought them only toil and deprivation." Among those on the "long and wearyful" journey were the private soldier returning from war to resume his fight with nature, the tenant under the lion's paw of his landlord, the weary housewife, and the oppressed farmer.

36 Goble, Paul and Dorothy. *Lone Bull's Horse Raid*. (I)
Bradbury Pr., 1973. 63p.

I wanted that beautiful black horse. My father tried to hold me back. I should have been satisfied with the one I had taken but I was young and, with Charging Bear beside me, I felt strong.

Lone Bull, a fourteen-year-old Oglala Sioux boy, joined his first horse raiding party against the Crows and gained honor for his bravery and generosity in this initiation into the life of a warrior. The husband and wife team of Paul and Dorothy Goble wrote with respect for Indian traditions and history. Paul Goble's illustrations were modeled after late nineteenth-century Plains Indian paintings.

37   Hager, Jean.   *The Whispering House.*   Steck, 1970.   **(I)**
181p.   op

What fantastic tales you must know, old house. Maybe you are whispering secrets . . . a whispering house.

After the death of their parents, Anne and her two brothers traveled to Union City, Kansas, to make their home with Uncle Julian. After a career on the stage, Uncle Julian had returned to the ancestral home built before the Civil War by Charles Owens, the children's great-great-grandfather. Rumor was that Owens had been a Confederate spy, a treasonable offense in "Union" Kansas. With the help of the whispering house, Anne found the truth and the evidence needed to vindicate her ancestor.

38   Hays, Wilma Pitchford.   *The Apricot Tree.*   **(J, S)**
Washburn, 1968.   152p.   op

No one can do so much for everyone, Joy, and have . . . time left for herself.

Joy Carter spent her life concentrating on helping her family face difficult situations and obtaining her degree from the University of Nebraska. A series of setbacks forced her father to relinquish his farm which made her dreams of college seem impossible. Each challenge was resolved, however, and Joy and her husband reached their educational goals. Joy's life is traced through the depression years until her tenth year of marriage.

39   Hays, Wilma Pitchford.   *Little Lone Coyote.*   Illus.   **(P, I)**
by Wesley Dennis.   Little, 1961.   34p.   op

Coyote was born wild and free. . . . He cannot forget freedom. Coyote's spirit withers if he is chained. He'd soon die.

Although coyotes do not roam the plains as freely in present-day Nebraska as they did in the days when settlement of the prairie was sparse, there were still enough people to make a large coyote hunt an annual event. Riding his pony home from school, Fred found a tiny coyote pup orphaned because its mother disappeared during the hunt. The problems Fred faced raising the wild coyote on a Nebraska sand-hills ranch provide an appealing story. Wesley Dennis' drawings add compassion and realism. Younger readers will enjoy this brief glimpse of life in modern Nebraska's ranch country.

40   Hays, Wilma Pitchford. *Little Yellow Fur.* Illus. by   (P)
          Richard Cuffari. (A Break-of-Day-Book) Coward,
          1973. 48p.

> "Play close to the house," her mother warned Susanna. "South Dakota is wild country."

Based on her childhood experiences on a 1913 homestead near the Rosebud Indian Reservation, Hays creates the story of blonde Susanna, called "Little Yellow Fur" by the Indians, and Terk, her Great Dane, the "Dog-big-as-a-pony." Mother feared the Indians who rode by on their ponies might kidnap her, but Susanna knew the Indians were her friends. This story is unusual for its treatment of Indian/white relationships.

41   Hoffine, Lyla. *Carol Blue Wing, What Is Your*   (J, S)
          Pleasure? McKay, 1967. 214p.

> My best friend, what is your pleasure?
> I say my future is my pleasure.

These words from an Indian song taught to Carol by her grandmother were significant to the young woman as she spent the summer before her senior year in college at home, making decisions about her future. As she focused on herself, she became aware of the conflicting values of some reservation Indians who were unable to live successfully either in their world or in white society.

42   Hoffine, Lyla. *The Eagle Feather Prize.* Illus. by   (I)
          Earl Lonsbury. McKay, 1962. 147p.   op

> "Eagle feathers yes!" Grandmother said scornfully. "His family will buy them. That is not the best. The best is to earn the right to have them."

Through his participation in the first 4-H Club on the Mandan Indian Reservation, Billy Youngbear unexpectedly earned the honored eagle-feather prize. The life-styles of three families are realistically portrayed. The Youngbears, a Mandan Indian family, live in contemporary society yet recognize the merits of both the Swift Runners, who prefer the traditional Indian ways, and the McKinnons, a modern white family.

43   Hoffine, Lyla. *Jennie's Mandan Bowl.* Illus. by   (I)
          Larry Toschik. Longmans, 1960. 105p.   op

17

Ask her [your grandmother] if she knows how to make pottery the way her people made it. I want to learn how to do it.

The teacher's words provoked a host of conflicting feelings in Jennie, a Mandan Indian girl. Although she loved her teacher, she did not want to learn Indian ways. She preferred the ways of white people. This sensitive portrayal shows how Jennie gained an appreciation of her Indian heritage and the realization that a person need not discard the old to profit from the new. The central theme of facing ethnic-minority difficulties is handled with sympathy and understanding.

44 Hoffine, Lyla. *Running Elk*. Illus. by Patricia   (I)
Boodell. Bobbs-Merrill, 1957. 108p.   op

"When will I learn enough to be a medicine man?" Running Elk wanted to know.

The fictional life of Running Elk, an Arikara boy who lived on the prairie banks of the Missouri River in what is now North Dakota, gives the reader a glimpse of life in an Indian village prior to Lewis and Clark's expedition. Running Elk had many difficulties in trying to prove to his family that he had achieved the qualities necessary to be a medicine man like his grandfather.

45 Holling, Holling C. *Tree in the Trail*. Houghton,   (I, J)
1942. 63p.

Ancient history coming to light—things the old tree had swallowed in her past!

A lone cottonwood sapling was discovered by an Indian boy who sought to protect it with rocks from destruction by the buffalo. It struggled and grew, giving shelter to Spaniards, Indians, hunters, and pioneers. Messages were posted in its trunk until a Kansas tornado uprooted it. As the tree was being carved into an ox yoke to go proudly into Santa Fe, its historic past was revealed by stone and iron arrowheads, slivers of steel, and a lead ball from a French trapper's smoothbore. The unique format includes outstanding illustrations by the author and factual marginal notes.

46 Hosford, Jessie. *An Awful Name to Live Up to*.   (I)
Illus. by Charles Geer. Meredith Pr., 1969. 187p.   op

Papa, I can't stand to live in this desolation any longer. I must get away from this awful country.

Mother was English, and she constantly appealed to her German husband to sell the Nebraska homestead and move back East. Papa was patient, and even the threat of prairie fire, the worry about cattle lost in the blizzard, and George's constant pranks, such as tying the horses' tails together, did not sway his determination to stay. This diary account of Julia Ward Howe Hoffman, affectionately called Little Diddit by her father, recounts the discouragements, yet final hope and security of life on a Nebraska farm.

47   Hosford, Jessie. *You Bet Your Boots I Can.*   Nelson,   (J, S)
         1971.   269p.

   My mother calls Nebraska a grim desolation, but Papa says it is beautiful.

Life on the Nebraska frontier at the turn of the century is vividly presented in the first person account of Julia Ward Howe Hoffman. Her struggle for an education was followed by a difficult experience teaching in a rural school with limited supplies and without a library. The author reveals her firsthand knowledge of pioneer life in this thought-provoking novel.

48   Hubbard, Margaret Ann.   *The Trouble on Shake-Rag*   (I)
         Creek.   Illus. by Carolyn Cather.   Doubleday, 1967.   op
         166p.

   "Donnie's always right about farm animals," Granny said firmly.

A twenty-six-year-old, mentally-retarded neighbor, Donnie, was implicated in some mysterious thefts in the community. Donnie's kind-hearted treatment of animals, including her pet wild rabbit, convinced eleven-year-old Becky of his innocence. The author's childhood experiences on a farm near the town of Souris, North Dakota, enabled her to create warm, believable characters in a farm community setting.

49   Hudson, Lois Phillips.   *The Bones of Plenty.*   Little,   (S)
         1962.   439p.   op

   After this morning's catastrophes, he felt more desperately far behind than ever.

Thus begins the novel of a tenant farm family in North Dakota during the early months of the New Deal when the consequences of the Wall Street crash reach the Dakotas. The story opens with the bank closing in February 1933, and continues to March 1934, when the impoverished Custer family packs its pitiful belongings into a trailer and heads for California. As Hudson notes, "it is hard for us now to believe that these things ever happened."

50   Hudson, Lois Phillips.   *Reapers of the Dust: A Prairie*   (S)
         Chronicle.   Little, 1964.   173p.   op

   The tub, refilled after we had emptied it for the stock, was standing in the corner of the kitchen next to the door. The snow in it was still heaped in a neat cone.

The quotation describes "The Cold Wave," one of the stories Lois Hudson tells about growing up on a North Dakota farm during the drought and depression of the 1930s. She recalls a Halloween prank, a child's gopher hunt, a poultry show, and the devastating tornado that finally drove her family westward to become migrant workers.

51   Hueston, Ethel.   *Calamity Jane of Deadwood Gulch.*   (S)
Bobbs-Merrill, 1937.   306p.   op

> He says to me, "Jane, you're a good pal to have around in time o' calamity like this."

Deadwood Gulch and its gold boom serve as the setting for this novel peopled with Indians, gamblers, prospectors, surveyors, bull-whackers, preachers, and a modicum of women. One of these characters is Calamity Jane, who continues to fascinate the present-day reader just as she did forty years ago when this novel was written. While the known facts of Jane's life are few, the author manages to trace Jane's gun-toting career from 1875 until her death in 1903. Jane's toughness is contrasted with the gentility of her friend Phoebe, daughter of an itinerant missionary. Through Phoebe's eyes Jane is seen as a diamond in the rough, the possessor of a kind and gentle heart.

52   Hueston, Ethel.   *Star of the West: The Romance of*   (S)
the Lewis and Clark Expedition.   Bobbs-Merrill,   op
1935.   364p.

> Always, forever after, her eager spirit would find rest from her harassed body through the sun-bright avenues of memory and hope.

Hueston explains in the foreword that this book was really written by six American heroes—Lewis and Clark, Floyd, Ordway, Whitehouse, and Gass—and that her work is merely a novelization of the original journals of the Lewis and Clark expedition. The Shoshoni Indian guide, Sacagawea, is the story's heroine. No fictional characters were introduced and much conversation was supplied verbatim from their texts. Footnotes and an appendix provide further proof of the story's authenticity.

53   Jackson, Charles Tenney.   *The Buffalo Wallow: A*   (J)
Prairie Boyhood.   Bobbs-Merrill, 1952.   253p.   op
(Paperback ed., Univ. of Nebraska Pr., 1967)

> The Waller was the spot gouged out by untold generations of buffalo as they rubbed their itchy backs into the under-sand.

In this first-person account of a boy's life in a treeless land, the buffalo wallow became a hideout, a last bastion in a land where the treeless prairie was facing the plow. The boys could go to the section-

20

corner of their ranch and find the surveyor's stake, so they were sure they lived in the middle of everything. They used their "Joggerfee" book to explore north, south, east, and west; and these adventures uncovered such things as a hangman's house, a lonely grave, and a mysterious murder. When the boys again visited their "Center of America," the prairie grass was gone and their land of mystery had become cornfields. This appealing picture depicts the lighter side of a boy's life on the prairie and is autobiographical in nature.

54 John, Alvin. *The Battle of the Wild Turkey and Other* (J, S)
  Tales. Atheneum, 1961. 241p. op

  Be with me for a little while in Old Nebraska.

Women are the central figures in several of the eight stories which form this collection. The title story is a humorous account of a successful hunt for an enormous turkey gobbler which ended in the liberation of one pioneer woman from male domination. In "The Long Way Round" a happy, independent couple reflect that the satisfying life does not necessarily require the amassing of great wealth. The story of Granny McBride is a heartwarming account which could spark an excellent discussion of the continuing problem of unfair treatment of senior citizens.

55 Johnson, Norma. *What Would We See?* Pheasant (P)
  Books, 1963. 33p. (Available through Kansas State op
  Reading Circle)

  What would we see if we were riding along—
  Riding along in the middle of Kansas?

A Kansas poem written by their teacher was the inspiration for the illustrations by second-grade students. The result is a charming, childlike book. Children respond to a variety of questions in order to determine that they could not see a kangaroo or an elephant on the Kansas plains, but they might see a pony or a "bouncy bounce bunny."

56 Keith, Harold. *The Bluejay Boarders.* Illus. by (I)
  Harold Berson. Crowell, 1972. 224p.

  "Bluejays," she thought, "are fascinating birds."

While visiting their grandmother at Meade, Kansas, for the summer, the three Barnes children, Susan, Joey, and Tom, adopted a family of infant bluejays, orphaned when Joey killed the mother with his slingshot. The feeding and care of the birds was time-consuming, but the children accepted the responsibility. One by one the birds died until only Jim, the largest and strongest, was left. Even he was abducted by

Beaky Callahan, a neighbor boy, who later returned him and became a family friend.

57 Laman, Russell. *Manifest Destiny.* Regnery, 1963. (S)
533p.

The endless cycles of toil for small profits became apparent early to Phil.

Spanning two wars and forty years of struggle, this story tells of John Phillip Garwood who came to Kansas in the 1880s after a financial loss in the stock market. He soon discovered that the soil was equally unpredictable and required patience that he did not have. The Populist Party became Garwood's hope for bettering his economic status, but through this involvement he neglected the land.

58 Lane, Neola Tracy. *Grasshopper Year.* Illus. by (I)
Dorothy Bayley Morse. Lippincott, 1960. 149p. op

The ground was pocked with holes showing the shapes of the beets and carrots and long icicle radishes.

Eddie, a Kansas farm boy of 1870, planned to spend his summer herding cattle at the Big Place. He was amazed at the lush green growth when he returned home for a brief vacation. However, the frightening cloud of grasshoppers soon destroyed everything. Vivid descriptions of the devastation and the Kansan's determination to survive should inspire greater understanding and respect for that period in Kansas history.

59 Lane, Rose Wilder. *Free Land.* Longmans, 1938. (S)
332p. op

As he stood, he was worth near fifteen hundred dollars, and Uncle Sam would give him a quarter-section of the best land on God's green footstool.

The incentive of free land in South Dakota beckoned nineteen-year-old David Beaton and his young bride. There they endured the hardships of extreme weather conditions, horse thieves, unfriendly Indians, and shrewd bankers. This moving novel of homesteading near Yankton provides a realistic picture of people with the courage and faith necessary for pioneering in the American West.

60 Lane, Rose Wilder. *Let the Hurricane Roar.* (J, S)
Longmans, 1933. 152p. (Reprint ed., McGraw-Hill, op
1976, under title *Young Pioneers*)

Air and sun and snow were the whole visible world—a world neither alive nor dead, and terrible because it was alien to life and death, and ignorant of them.

This simple story involves two young pioneers whose baby is born in their homestead dugout during a blizzard. Although their dreams of success were shattered by a grasshopper plague, their courage and determination enabled them to endure the fury of winter and the loneliness of separation.

61   Laughlin, Florence. *The Seventh Cousin.* Illus. by   (I)
         Sheila Greenwald. Macmillan, 1966. 160p.

> He could almost hear the satisfied sigh of the big old Truelove Mansion as it settled back on its foundations.

Dedicated to "the wonderful children of Lincoln," the setting for this simple mystery is an old Lincoln, Nebraska, home which a monkey has inherited. The Carter family moves into apartment number five, and the children become involved in the attempt to thwart the plan of the seventh cousin to steal the monkey and thus inherit the estate. The unexpected arrival of the granddaughter complicates the situation, but the mystery is solved. The plot moves swiftly and should appeal to young mystery lovers.

62   Le Grand. *Cats for Kansas.* Abingdon, 1948. 40p.   (P)
                                                                      op

> All the settlers in Kansas want a cat. And there are no cats in Kansas.

Since many of the early settlers longed for the peaceful purring of cats, Old Gabe decided to go back East and bring some back. He acquired the cats; but before he reached home, he encountered many tall-tale adventures. Fortunately for the settlers, the trader accomplished his mission. Humorous illustrations highlight the action.

63   Lenski, Lois. *Little Sioux Girl.* (Roundabout   (I)
         America) Lippincott, 1958. 128p.

> "Now you are truly a little Sioux girl!" said Grandma.

Day-to-day living on the Standing Rock Indian Reservation required that Indian children go to school and live according to the times. Yet Grandma's idea of being truly Sioux was dressing as she once did and sharing Indian toys and activities. Lenski's purpose in this work is to help children examine a specific way of life.

64   Lenski, Lois. *Prairie School.* (Regional Stories)   (I)
         Lippincott, 1951. 196p. (Paperback ed., Dell, 1967)

> "If you cry," said Miss Martin, "I'm going to cry too. We'll all sit down and cry, but the storm will go on just the same. . . . We may as well be cheerful and make the best of it."

23

Lois Lenski wrote this story on location in McLaughlin, South Dakota, in 1950 while viewing the prairie for the first time, sleeping on a cot at Maple Leaf School, and sharing the children's lunches and experiences. This is her tribute to all rural school teachers and to the children who rode horseback to school, spoke pieces at Christmas programs, and had to stay at the schoolhouse for days at a time during raging blizzards.

65   McNeely, Marian Hurd.   *The Jumping-Off Place.*   (I, J)
        Illus. by William Siegel.   Longmans, 1929.   308p.   op

> Dakota! You aren't planning to go out to the Jumping-Off Place to visit that homestead?

When their Uncle Jim died, the orphaned Linville children followed his last wishes and moved from Illinois to his homestead in Tripp County on the Rosebud Indian Reservation. In spite of their Aunt Jule's assessment that it was a God-forsaken place, they determined to hold down the claim for the required fourteen months to obtain title to the land. Their indomitable spirit allowed them to triumph over claim jumpers, blizzards, droughts, grasshoppers, and poverty.

66   Manfred, Frederick.   *The Golden Bowl.*   Webb,   (S)
        1944.   226p.   (Reprint ed., Univ. of New Mexico Pr.,   op
        1976)

> They say [this land's] a dust bowl now. . . . But I can close my eyes and see the golden bowl it's been . . . an' it'll be full a gold again. I know.

Maury Grant hitchhiked across South Dakota in the dust-bowl year of 1934. His desire for the open road and an illusory job in the Black Hills is contrasted to the stubborn optimism of Pa and Ma Thor who are certain that someday the rains will come again. Their contagious belief causes Maury to return from his wanderings and provides the basis of his hope for the future on the land. Frederick Manfred based this novel on his own experiences during the depression years.

67   Meigs, Cornelia.   *The Willow Whistle.*   Illus. by E.   (I)
        Boyd Smith.   Macmillan, 1931.   144p.

> "Mary Anne!" he shouted with all his might, and in answer the sound came again, the clear call of a willow whistle.

At her father's trading station in newly settled prairie country, two friends helped Mary Anne overcome her shyness. Eric Thorveg, a blonde Norwegian boy, taught her to make a willow whistle. Gray Eagle, a Dakota Indian Chief, befriended her and aided her escape from the enemy Arickarees. The story closes with the unsuccessful attempt of the Arickarees to burn the schoolhouse and destroy the magic signs in the white man's books.

68   Mohler, Marjorie M.   *Brave Heritage.*   Exposition,   (I, J)
          1963.   222p.

> It is here we belong. Here on this beloved land that is ours by the very toil of our hands.

In an English settlement near Wakefield, Kansas, during the post-Civil War period, a family of English gentry struggled to cope with severe weather and grasshoppers. The establishment of a profitable fruit farm ultimately proved that hard work is more rewarding than a life of leisure. The author drew on stories recalled from childhood.

69   Murphy, Robert.   *Wild Geese Calling.*   Illus. by John   (I)
          Kaufman.   Dutton, 1966.   96p.

> The river bluffs, high and sculptured, familiar from the past, stirred a feeling of homecoming in both of them.

A pair of wild Canada geese migrated from the Aransas National Wildlife Refuge in Texas to Lostwood National Wildlife Refuge in North Dakota. On their southward journey in the fall the gander was wounded by a hunter. Rescued by a lonely boy, he was cared for during the winter. After his recovery and release, he found his mate again.

70   Neihardt, John G.   *When the Tree Flowered.*   (S)
          Macmillan, 1951.   248p.   (Paperback ed., Univ. of   op
          Nebraska Pr., 1970; Pocket Books, 1973)

> You shall breathe the dust of battles, counting many coups, and shall not be hurt.

This fictional autobiography of Eagle Voice, a Sioux warrior of the latter 1800s, incorporates such actual historical events as Custer's Last Stand with legends and accounts of tribal customs. Buffalo hunts, raiding parties, and sun dances are treated accurately and sympathetically. Neither caricatures nor stereotypes, Neihardt's Indians, depicted in the colorful arena of the frontier, are real people with deep feelings.

71   Parks, Gordon.   *The Learning Tree.*   Harper, 1963.   (J, S)
          303p.   (Paperback ed., Fawcett-World, 1975)

> "I've got to prove somethin'—to myself."

Newt, an inexperienced adolescent of the 1920s in Cherokee Flats, Kansas, struggled to survive. He encountered violence, sexual experiences, and close brushes with death in the ghetto. Each new lesson gained from the "learning tree" helped Newt discover his role in life.

72   Reese, John Henry.   *Big Mutt.*   Illus. by Rod Ruth.   (I, J)
      Westminster, 1952.   190p.   (Paperback ed., Archway,   op
      nd)

> Twenty lonely, grieving hours in a coyote's den had stripped away
> those two years of tameness like so much excess fat.

Born and raised in New York City, a large mongrel dog was aban-
doned by his owners in the Badlands during a blizzard. Forced to survive in an alien setting, he became a tribulation to the sheep ranchers
who were determined to kill him. Dwight Jerome, with his unswerving
faith in "Big Mutt," prevented his destruction. Love and understanding
of animals are well depicted.

73   Reilly, Robert T.   *Massacre at Ash Hollow.*   Illus. by   (J, S)
      Dirk Gringhuis.   (Catholic Treasury Books) Bruce,   op
      1960.   156p.

> It's my belief that Omaha City'll be a right smart place one day.
> Right smart.

Jamie McWilliam's opinion of Omaha City in 1855 differed greatly
from that of the captain of the riverboat, *Washington City*. His father's
hatred of the wild Nebraska territory had influenced his son to such a
degree that Jamie saw no merit in the new land. After his father's supposed murder by the Sioux, Jamie leaves Omaha City on a cattle drive
for the army in hopes of finding his father's killer. In the process of dis-
covering who the murderer is, Jamie also finds himself. While describing the settlement of the new territory, the author, with sensitivity and
understanding, portrays the gradual debasement of the Indian tribes by
the whites. Objectivity is evidenced in the author's attempt to present
both points of view in this portrayal of persons who actually lived
during the era.

74   Rock, Gail.   *Addie and the King of Hearts.*   Illus. by   (I, J)
      Charles McVickers.   Knopf, 1976.   85p.   (Paperback
      ed., 1977)

> I just want to be old enough to do what I want.

Growing up has never been easy, and in Clear River, Nebraska, in
1949, Addie Mills was certainly having her problems. Too old to be
considered a child and too young to be the "sophisticate" she would
like, thirteen-year-old Addie finds herself with a crush on Mr. Daven-
port, her teacher. Undaunted by the teasings of her friends and father,
she manages to survive the pain and frustration of being left out. Writing with compassion and understanding, Gail Rock paints a detailed
picture of rural Nebraska. Charles McVickers's illustrations add clarity

to the story. Other books with the same setting are *The Thanksgiving Treasure* (Knopf, 1974), *The House without a Christmas Tree* (Knopf, 1974), and *A Dream for Addie* (Knopf, 1975).

75   Rock, Gail.   *The Thanksgiving Treasure.*   Illus. by   (P, I)
      Charles C. Gehm.   Knopf, 1974.   90p.   (Paperback
      ed., Bantam, 1976)

> Sometimes I would come into the barn and Rehnquist would be there, rubbing Treasure's nose and talking softly to her.

Addie loved horses, and on a forbidden visit to eccentric Mr. Rehnquist's rundown farm, she discovered his pinto horse, Treasure. Afraid to ask her father's permission because he considered Rehnquist an enemy, Addie was forced to sneak Thanksgiving dinner to the old man. A touching friendship developed between Addie and Rehnquist as Addie exercised Treasure. After the old man's death, Addie's family discovered the real meaning of Thanksgiving. The characters in this story, based on the author's own experiences in a Nebraska town during the 1940s, are portrayed with realism and humor.

76   Rolfsrud, Erling Nicolai.   *Boy from Johnny Butte.*   (I)
      Illus. by Lee Mero.   Augsburg, 1956.   122p.   op

> Axel Kittilson, he ain't good company for your son, Revrun' Steen. Always a free thinker. . . . Von't set foot in Church.

Coming from Minneapolis to the frontier of western North Dakota was a significant change for the minister, his wife, and son Karl. Karl liked Axel because he was the only person in the area with a car and a tractor; and he promised to teach Karl to drive them. Although Axel was always kind to his neighbors, he felt church and God were taboo subjects. Kindness, understanding, and love form the basis for the attitude change that transpired.

77   Rolfsrud, Erling Nicolai.   *Gopher Tails for Papa.*   (I)
      Illus. by Herman Fay, Jr.   Augsburg, 1951.   86p.   op

> The women sitting nearby gasped in astonishment as he (Sven) dumped the gopher tails into the church collection.

The little prairie church needed an organ, and each gopher tail had a bounty value of three cents. Based on historical incidents, Sven and his preacher family recreate a life on the Dakota prairie during the settlement of the Midwest. A variety of experiences ensued, from an Indian, garbed in a red nightgown, entering church and quietly walking away with an accordian to the excitement of a raging prairie fire.

78   Rolfsrud, Erling Nicolai.   *The Tiger-Lily Years.*   (I, J, S)
      Lantern Books, 1975.   103p.

So he sat for hours with the soft mud oozing between his toes . . . and while his fingers busied themselves, busier still was his mind that pondered his chances of ever becoming a man, a real man.

A young sensitive, fatherless boy faced life in western North Dakota. Although his family had little money, its members possessed solidarity, optimism, and strong religious convictions which gave them strength. This authentic and nostalgic view of farm life in the 1920s was based on the author's own experiences.

79   Rolvaag, Ole Edvart. *Giants in the Earth: A Saga of*   (S)
      the Prairie. Harper, 1927. 465p. (Paperback ed.,
      1965)

> Day after day the same . . . evening after evening. Strangely still the days . . . the evenings more mysteriously quiet .How could one lift one's voice against such silence!

Generally recognized as a classic of American frontier life, Rolvaag's novel reflects his Scandinavian heritage as well as his desire to tell of the immigrant's part in building a new nation. Per Hansa and his wife Beret were among a small group of Norwegian farmers who trekked from Minnesota to Dakota Territory in 1873. They built sod huts and broke the prairie for crops, but the environment was cruel. Per Hansa, ambitious, full of strength and courage, is a symbol of the true pioneer spirit, but Beret is lonely, frightened, and overwhelmed by "the infinitude surrounding her." Rolvaag's title was taken from Genesis 6:4: "There were giants in the earth in those days . . . mighty men which were of old, men of renown."

80   Rounds, Glen. *The Blind Colt.* Holiday, 1960. unp.   (I)

> They sat on their horses and watched awhile and admired the colt. "Purty as a picture, ain't he, Uncle Torwal?" said Whitey. "Reckon we better take him home so the wolves won't get him?"

A wild colt, born blind in the Badlands of South Dakota, became the Sunday horse of a ten-year-old-boy. Sagebrush, chokecherries, rain-gullied buttes, and alkali flats of the Badlands are the background of this boy-and-his-horse story in which the daily happenings on a ranch are highlighted. The same characters appear in the author's *Stolen Pony* (Holiday, 1948) and the books of the "Whitey" series, including *Whitey Ropes and Rides* (Holiday, 1956), and *Whitey's First Roundup* (Holiday, 1960).

81   Sandoz, Mari. *The Horsecatcher.* Westminster,   (J, S)
      1957. 192p.

> This one we know about is white . . . white as the snows that live in the mountains, but it is known that he cannot be caught.

To become a horsecatcher for his people rather than a warrior, the young Cheyenne defied tradition. The Indian religion, folkways, and customs influenced Young Elk, who courageously sought to live by peaceful principles. The book is dedicated to "the two great Cheyennes named Elk River, both council chiefs and peace men, one Keeper of the Sacred Arrows of the Cheyenne Indians, the other the greatest horse-catcher of all the High Plains."

82   Sandoz, Mari. *Miss Morissa.*   McGraw-Hill, 1955.   (S)
         249p. (Reprint ed., Hastings, 1975)   op

> Morissa Kirk had other patients, as far away as Pratt's and up the trail, men who were desperately ill too, one died almost before she got to him.

The life of a woman doctor in early Camp Clarke, Nebraska, was difficult, but Morissa Kirk's problems were compounded by the constant reminders of her illegitimate birth. Grass fires, smallpox, diphtheria, the death of her friend while he tried to rescue her beloved Appaloosa, and her unfortunate marriage to the outlaw Eddie Ellis are among the high points in the narrative. When she refused to help Eddie in crime, he set fire to her hospital. All feared she would leave; but as they brought a petition requesting her to stay, they found her borrowing money to rebuild. In addition to its readable style, young people of today will appreciate the independence which this woman doctor exhibited in a male-dominated society.

83   Sandoz, Mari. *Sandhill Sundays and Other Recollec-*   (J, S)
         tions.   North American Review, 1930.   165p.   op
         (Reprint ed., Univ. of Nebraska Pr., 1970)

> It was this offer of free land that drew my father, Old Jules Sandoz, west to a homestead in the unorganized region that was to become Sheridan County, Nebraska.

The setting for nine of the ten selections in this volume, written between 1929 and 1965, is the sandhills of northwestern Nebraska. The characters are friends and neighbors, and Sandoz admits that her stories could have resulted from the childhood of any homestead youth. Many children worked twelve to fourteen hours daily from March to November. Neighbors were the source of security and pleasure, as indicated in "The Christmas of the Phonograph Records." People from miles around heard of the Edison phonograph in Jules Sandoz's house, and came to share the music—and the Sandoz food. A Sandoz chronology is included to put the stories in perspective. The appealing style will help the reader picture the blizzards and privations which tested the courage of the early Nebraska pioneer.

84   Sandoz, Mari.   *The Story Catcher*.   Illus. by Elsie   (I)
      J. McCorkell.   Westminster, 1963.   175p.   (Paper-   op
      back ed., Grosset, nd)

   The picture is the rope that ties memory solidly to the stake of
   truth.

Lance brings a young Ree boy into the village and faces many
dangers in his desire to protect him. After numerous setbacks because
of impulsive acts, including captivity by the Crows, Lance becomes
Story Catcher, a picture maker of the deeds of his people, and gains the
right to become Blue Dawn's suitor. Sandoz, a noted Nebraska author,
presents an exciting tale of the life of a young Sioux boy.

85·   Sandoz, Mari.   *Winter Thunder*.   Westminster,   (I, J)
      1954.   61p.   (Paperback ed., Scholastic, 1972)

   Dawn came early that eighth day, but it seemed that nothing could
   be left alive in the cold whiteness of the earth that was only frozen
   scarves of snow flung deep and layered over themselves.

A courageous young school teacher led her seven pupils to the
protection of a willow clump when the school bus was wrecked during
the blizzard. For eight days, with only their school lunches for nourish-
ment, the group miraculously endured fifty inches of snow and a tem-
perature registering 38° below zero. This amazing tale of survival was
based on the adventures of the author's niece during the blizzard of
January 1949.

86   Seibert, Jerry.   *Sacajawea: Guide to Lewis and Clark*.   (I)
      Illus. by Lorence Bjorklund.   (Piper Books) Houghton,   op
      1960.   192p.

   Remember landmarks—big things like the curve of a peak against
   the sky, and small things like the crooked branch of a tree.

The brave Indian woman, named for the great trumpeter swan,
and the courageous men of the Lewis and Clark expedition were the
first Americans to cross the Rocky Mountains and reach the Pacific
Ocean. Based on the journals of Lewis and Clark, this fictional biography covers Sacajawea's life from her birth and childhood in the Rockies
until September 23, 1806, when the expedition safely returned to St.
Louis. Lorence Bjorklund's illustrations and maps are well suited to the
text.

87   Sneve, Virginia Driving Hawk.   *Betrayed*.   Holiday,   (J)
      1974.   125p.

   Many of my people call me and my followers crazy and even
   traitors for going to the rescue of whites. We are known as the "Fool

Soldiers," but we are not ashamed of the name. Is it foolish to do a good thing?

Destitute, half-starved, and angry with the United States government for unkept treaties, the Indians killed and maimed white settlers of the Minnesota Valley and took many women and children captive during the Santee Indian uprising of 1862. The captives wandered through the Dakota Territory before their rescue by young Charger, a Teton brave, and his friends. This realistic story portrays kindness and understanding on both sides. A glossary of Indian words is included.

88 Sneve, Virginia Driving Hawk. *High Elk's Treasure.*   (I)
Illus. by Oren Lyons. Holiday, 1972. 96p.

> "Star is gone, Star is gone." . . . How could the herd begin again when part of its hope was wandering, lost along the creek?

Thirteen-year-old Joe High Elk had heard the tale of the High Elk horses all his life. His great-grandfather had returned from the Battle of the Little Big Horn with a scrawny palomino mare which, when bred to a golden quarter horse from the agency corral, produced the first of a line of famous horses. Joe allowed the prized young filly, Star, to escape and feared his father's dreams for rebuilding the herd were doomed. However, the rescue of Star from the wild horse catchers and the discovery of High Elk's treasure, a pictographic record of the Battle of the Little Big Horn hidden in a cave for one hundred years, offered new hope for Joe's family. A phonetic glossary of Dakota words is included. Sneve's own childhood on South Dakota's Rosebud Reservation provides background for her stories.

89 Sypher, Lucy Johnston. *Cousins and Circuses.* Illus.   (I)
by Ray Abel. Atheneum, 1974. 250p.

> "Wales isn't wicked just because it's different. It's not. I know it's not!" Lucy refused to give in.

Based on the author's childhood experiences in the North Dakota village of Wales, this sequel to *The Edge of Nowhere* is the story of Lucy and the events that highlighted the summer of 1916. Although Lucy worried about Wales being a wicked place in which to live, she found the county fair in Langdon, the traveling Chautauqua, and the five hundred-mile trip to Minneapolis more worthy of her attention. Frontier life during this period is convincingly portrayed.

90 Sypher, Lucy Johnston. *The Edge of Nowhere.*   (I)
Illus. by Ray Abel. Atheneum, 1972. 211p.

> "Nothing ever happens here. Nothing happened in 1915 and you just wait—nothing will happen in 1916," said Lucy in disgust. "But I just wish it would."

Sixth-grader Lucy Johnston was lonely and bored until she had responsibilities as a fire-watcher, teacher, housekeeper during a blizzard, and protector when a tornado threatened. In one year, life in Lucy's town seemed to change. The author portrays frontier life in Wales, North Dakota, based on her own childhood experiences.

91   Sypher, Lucy Johnston. *The Spell of the Northern*   (I)
       Lights. Illus. by Ray Abel. Atheneum, 1975. 251p.

    There before her and overhead glowed the strange rays of light, shifting and flickering, illuminating the whole wide prairie sky.

Continuing the account of Lucy's childhood in Wales, North Dakota, begun in *The Edge of Nowhere* and *Cousins and Circuses,* this work emphasizes Lucy's success in conquering her many fears. The routine of village life for Lucy was interrupted by a blizzard, Halloween, grain elevator fires, her mother's pregnancy, and the vivid panorama of the Northern Lights.

92   Sypher, Lucy Johnston. *The Turnabout Year.* Illus.   (I, J)
       by Ray Abel. Atheneum, 1976. 216p.

    By now summer was ending, and Lucy felt everything else was ending also.

In the last book in the series about Lucy Johnston's family in the frontier town of Wales, North Dakota, Lucy predicts on December 31, 1916, that she will leave Wales before another year is gone. The year's wait is filled with adventures. Mother has a baby, war is declared, and Lucy takes the state examinations. Lucy's prediction comes true in the climax of this readable tale from a series based on the author's own childhood.

93   Taylor, Don Alonzo. *Old Sam, Thoroughbred*   (I)
       Trotter. Illus. by Lorence F. Bjorklund. Follett,   op
       1955. 160p.

    You just can't beat Old Sam. . . . He's a thoroughbred trotting horse, he is.

The author recorded his boyhood adventures as a Dakota Territory pioneer in the 1880s with the purpose of sharing these experiences with his children. His daughter, a teacher, read the stories to her pupils; and their enthusiasm led her to seek a publisher. Memories of the emigrant train from Illinois, homesteading, blizzards, and potato thieves are authentically described. Old Sam's feat in the Fourth of July trotting race provided the story's exciting climax. *Old Sam and the Horse Thieves* (Follett, 1967) is a sequel to this tale.

94   Taylor, Ross McLaury. *We Were There on the*   (I, J)
        Chisholm Trail.   Illus. by Charles Banks Wilson.   op
        (We Were There . . .) Grosset, 1957.   176p.

   Always Chisholm's signs and markers were there just ahead of them, pointing the way and guiding them.

   Lance Calhoun had his own horse, a new saddle, a carbine, a bed-roll, and a tarpaulin as he rode the Chisholm Trail with the Box C outfit toward Abilene, Kansas. Before the cattle drive headed by Lance's father reached the end of the trail, Lance got a new .44 Colt pistol and made friends with a spooky steer. The working side of a cattle drive is well portrayed.

95   Taylor, Ross McLaury. *We Were There on the Santa*   (I, J)
        Fe Trail.   Illus. by Albert Orbaan.   (We Were   op
        There . . .) Grosset, 1960.   176p.

   It was a long trail anyway you cut it.

   Young Mitch Ford traveled with his family from Virginia to Westport (Kansas City) on the Missouri River and from there to Santa Fe via the Santa Fe Trail. Beginning with the outfitting of the wagon train in Westport, the trip was one of excitement, danger, and adventure for Mitch. Outlaws, Indians, prairie fire, runaway horses, buffalo, and breakdowns were all a part of his life on the trail. Black-and-white illustrations enhance the text.

96   Tomerlin, John. *The Fledgling.*   Dutton, 1968.   (J, S)
        188p.

   One moment, it was a black speck against the lowering sun, the next, a shining white bird with wings of flame.

   Young Richard Newman watched the plane as though in a dream, then set off toward the El Dorado, Kansas, airport to see for himself. He became involved with the Tomkins International Air Show and learned to fly the blue-and-white Cessna despite the objections of his parents. Rich matured as he found new friends, new confidence, and a new freedom through flying. The adventurous experiences of early barn-stormers and stunt pilots are featured.

97   Trump, Fred. *Uphill into the Sun.*   Naylor, 1973.   (S)
        213p.

   Our state motto is my prayer—"To the Stars Through Difficulties."

   Born in Manchester, England, in 1850, Sarah Donnelly was raised in a middle-class home. She married Samuel Woolley in 1870 and moved to Kansas where he had a homestead. Her life in Kansas was difficult as she was not prepared for the hardships of weather, Indians, and daily drudgery. Sarah also discovered she had a self-centered husband who proved unfaithful. After sixteen years of marriage and the birth of eight children, she divorced Samuel and raised the family alone. This story of an indomitable woman is based on family letters and journals.

98   Turnbull, Roderick. *More Maple Hill Stories.*   (I, J, S)
         Lowell Pr., 1974. 309p.

> Sometimes I think the difference between now and what some people like to refer to as the good old days is cream.

This record of small-town life in the early 1900s is nostalgically presented by a skillful storyteller who recalls his boyhood in Maple Hill, Kansas. The appeal of this record of an era in history is increased by colored illustrations, originally on canvas, that capture the spirit of the period and complement the text.

99   Veglahn, Nancy. *Follow the Golden Goose.* Illus.   (I, J)
         by Milton Johnson.   Addison-Wesley, 1970. 171p.   op

> Take 'em to Deadwood and sell 'em.

Maybe it was not fourteen-year-old Neb Walters who brought the first load of cats to Deadwood from Bismarck, but it might have been. This story of Neb and his father in search of the goose that laid the golden egg during the 1876 Black Hills gold rush seems plausible. Cats, which brought $10 each, provided more certainty of profit than did fraudulent treasure maps of nonexistent gold fields. The text makes the reader cognizant that carpenters and other service people were vital for the existence of mining towns.

100 Wellman, Manly Wade. *Frontier Reporter.*   (J, S)
         Washburn, 1969. 148p.   op

> Those were practical men, but they had thought and planned and worked with utter unselfishness.

When Hugh Buckner began work as a reporter on the *Spring Creek Banner* in 1889, the burning issue of the day was the site of the county seat. Spring Creek and Grove City, its rival, were using the newspapers to wage a verbal battle. Thus, Hugh was called upon to be reporter, printer, and fighter. The political struggle, the finding of bones of extinct animals, and the opportunity to know Jan O'Connor, the editor's daughter, made an interesting year for Hugh.

101   Wilder, Laura Ingalls.   *By the Shores of Silver Lake.*   (I, J, S)
Illus. by Garth Williams.   Harper, 1953.   290p.
(Paperback ed., 1973)

  "And best of all Caroline, we're among the very first out here,"
said Pa. "We've got the pick of the land for our homestead."

The Ingalls family left Plum Creek when Pa became paymaster
for the railroad in Dakota Territory. They had a chance to pick up 160
acres of land "just by living on it." When the railroad camp broke up in
the fall, they were alone until spring's onrush of new settlers. Pa filed
on his homestead claim "south of where the lake joins Big Slough"
and near the townsite (De Smet, South Dakota). There they built a
shanty, and the family moved in.

102   Wilder, Laura Ingalls.   *The First Four Years.*   Illus.   (I, J, S)
by Garth Williams.   Harper, 1971.   134p.   (Paperback
ed., 1973)

  Laura and Manly were married for better or worse, for richer or
poorer.

During their first four years of marriage Laura and Manly experienced joy with the birth of their daughter, sadness with the death
of their son, and hardships with one crop failure following another.
Although fire destroyed their home, courage and love for the land gave
them faith for the future. The manuscript for this ninth *Little House*
book was discovered among the author's papers after her death.

103   Wilder, Laura Ingalls.   *Little House on the Prairie.*   (I, J, S)
Illus. by Garth Williams.   Harper, 1953.   334p.
(Paperback ed., 1973)

  She liked the enormous sky . . . the wind, and the land that you
couldn't see to the end of.

After the Ingalls family left the big woods in Wisconsin, they
traveled many days before finding a place to settle. On their home site
Indians were frequently seen nearby; and at night howling wolves
frightened the girls. Pa discovered that he had unknowingly settled in
government territory set aside for the Indians, and they were forced to
leave the little house on the Kansas prairie.

104   Wilder, Laura Ingalls.   *Little Town on the Prairie.*   (I, J, S)
Illus. by Garth Williams.   Harper, 1953.   304p.
(Paperback ed., 1973)

  Quickly Laura multiplied in her head. . . . She might earn fifteen
dollars, maybe even twenty, to help send Mary to college.

Laura got her first job in town helping to make men's shirts and felt satisfied that she could help out. By fall Mary was able to go to a college for the blind. During the winter months Laura and her family lived in town. Church activities and Saturday evening literaries occupied their time. The spring and summer months were spent working the family homestead.

105 Wilder, Laura Ingalls. *The Long Winter.* Illus. by   (I, J, S)
Garth Williams. Harper, 1953. 334p. (Paperback
ed., 1973)

"Heap, big snow, big wind. . . . Many moons," the Indian said. He held up four fingers, then three fingers. Seven fingers, seven months; blizzards for seven months.

The Ingalls family moved from their homestead claim to town (De Smet, South Dakota) to escape the hard winter ahead. As the Indian had predicted, the blizzards came. Because all the coal in town was gone, Pa made trips to the claim during the few clear days to bring back straw to burn. Since no trains were able to break through the snow to bring in more supplies, many people lived on bread and tea. Then one day the snow stopped, the sun shone, and the train came!

106 Wilder, Laura Ingalls. *These Happy Golden Years.*   (I, J, S)
Illus. by Garth Williams. Harper, 1953. 288p.
(Paperback ed., 1973)

Laura did not say anything. . . . She was on her way to teach school. Only yesterday she was a schoolgirl; now she was a school teacher.

Sixteen-year-old Laura was determined to become a teacher so that she might help keep Mary in the college for the blind. Teaching was difficult, the home where she boarded was depressing, and she was extremely homesick. On Friday afternoons Almanzo Wilder drove her the twelve miles home to spend weekends with her family. When the first term was over, Almanzo continued to see Laura. Two years later they were married.

107 Williams, Jeanne. *Coyote Winter.* Norton, 1965.   (I, J)
206p.   op

He didn't want spring to come. Talt would go then, back to the far territories and Wind River.

Fall brought the wild geese flying south over the Kansas prairie. It also brought home Whit Matthews' half-brother Talt, with his string of trading ponies. Whit's routine of helping Aunt Callie in the soddy and delivering Pa's weekly newspaper was interrupted by the arrival of Talt, who loved a carefree existence. Besides getting his own pony,

Whit found and tamed a wild coyote pup, Honey. In addition, he helped Pa and Talt overcome the bitterness that separated them.

108 Williams, Jeanne. *Freedom Trail.* Putnam, 1973.   (J)
156p.

> Many antislavery people feared that slave-owning Missourians would settle in Kansas long enough to vote it into the Union as a slave state.

Jared Hall, shocked by his father's death at the hands of pro-slavery men, found himself facing adult responsibilities in the Kansas Territory during pre-Civil War days. The friendship between Jared and Mark, a young Indian boy, grew as they became involved in the activities of the Underground Railroad and the turmoil in the Lawrence area. The hardships suffered by those who hoped to remain neutral is given special emphasis.

109 Williams, Jeanne. *Oh, Susanna!* Illus. by Albert   (J, S)
Orbaan. Putnam, 1963. 222p.   op

> That's the only way to stand this place. Think of what it can be.

Susanna Parks, her father, brother, and sister moved from St. Louis to the prairies of Kansas to homestead. The problems they faced were often heartbreaking. It took courage to live in a house built of sod, enduring cold, heat, dampness, sickness, and lack of luxuries. At seventeen Susanna was forced to assume the responsibilities of womanhood. Her experiences led to the discovery that hope was an essential element for prairie living.

110 Williams, Jeanne. *Winter Wheat.* Putnam, 1975.   (I, J)
157p.

> Almost two thousand Russian Mennonites came to Topeka that fall.

The pacifist Mennonites of German descent who came to Kansas in 1874 after fleeing Czarist Russia were a courageous people. Their precious seeds for winter wheat were to have great influence on the future of Kansas. This fictional account emphasizes the Landers family's strong faith and determination. Sixteen-year-old Cobie took a son's place beside her father in the fields. Cobie's love for her new home grew as she matured during their first year, and she promised to marry their newfound friend, Stede Martin.

111 Winther, Sophus Keith. *Take All to Nebraska.*   (S)
Macmillan, 1936. 305p. (Paperback ed., Univ. of   op
Nebraska Pr., 1976)

> Now this, at last, is all that I could ever have asked for.

Peter Grimsen's family came to America from Denmark seeking land that promised a home for the future. However, the poor soil of

New England, coupled with the prejudice directed at the Danish settlers, was enough to send them west to Nebraska. Here they found
many of the same obstacles, yet the land itself provided an incentive.
They believed that hard work would produce a good life. This story
of the Grimsens is a sensitive record of the frustrating yet challenging
existence of Nebraska's Danish settlers.

112 Wyatt, Geraldine. *Buffalo Gold.* Illus. by E. A.   (I, J)
     Furman. Longmans, 1948. 184p.   op
       The wheat made a whispering sound in the wind.

Fifteen-year-old Anson Hull was an idealistic dreamer, but he
had the determination to work tirelessly to make his dreams reality.
His strong love of the land kept him from becoming discouraged by
drought, prairie fires, and blizzards. Exciting hunts for wild horses and
buffaloes and a unique friendship with the Indians highlight the action.
Of interest to any age but especially suitable for young readers is this
story of the Mennonites' famous Turkey Red wheat.

113 Yates, Elizabeth. *Carolina's Courage.* Illus. by   (P, I)
     Nora S. Unwin. Dutton, 1964. 94p.
       She saw a flat and waiting land, laced with slow-moving creeks.

As the Putnam family left their New Hampshire farm by covered
wagon to seek land in the newly-opened Nebraska Territory, Caroline
chose her doll Lyddy as the one treasure she could take with her. On
the trail she replaces Lyddy with a hide doll in a gesture of friendship
to an Indian girl. In a surprising turn of events, the trade insures
Caroline's family safe-conduct to their new home. Black-and-white
illustrations enhance this simple, heartwarming story.

FOLKTALES

114 Beath, Paul R., comp. *Febold Feboldson: Tall Tales*   (J, S)
     from the Great Plains. Illus. by Lynn Trank. Univ.   op
     of Nebraska Pr., 1948. 124p. (Paperback ed., 1962)
       The legendary Swede lives again in these tales of the Great Plains.

Told primarily through the recollections of his great-nephew,
Bergstrom Stromberg, the hectic career of Swedish Febold Feboldson
is outlined as he tangles with droughts, floods, and tornadoes, averting
near crises through his quick thinking. Inventor of the bicycle, adviser
to the Union Pacific Railroad, and friend of Paul Bunyan, this ingen-
ious hero discovers creative solutions to numerous problems. When

fishermen in the Dismal River have trouble catching dogfish, he advises them to whistle. When rain is needed, Febold skillfully shoots a passing cloud. The short, snappy style of these humorous anecdotes should delight the reader.

115 Bierhorst, John, ed.   *The Ring in the Prairie: A*   (I, J)
Shawnee Legend.   Illus. by Leo and Diane Dillon.
Dial, 1970.   36p.   (Paperback ed., 1976)

Waupee spread his wings and, followed by his wife and son, descended with the other birds to the earth.

Waupee, a young hunter, discovered a mysterious ring on the prairie and was determined to find its secret. He hid and saw a basket carrying twelve beautiful sisters descend to the center of the ring. As he listened to the beautiful music and watched the maidens, he fell in love with the youngest. The romance which followed spanned heaven and earth. Unique, full-color illustrations capture the spirit of the tale.

116 Botkin, Benjamin A., ed.   *A Treasury of Western*   (S)
Folklore.   Crown, 1951.   613p.   (Rev. ed., 1975)   op

We hanged Jim for stealing a horse, but come to find out he didn't do it, so I guess the joke's on us.

Anecdotes, tall tales, yarns, humorous stories, local legends, folktales, and traditions are featured in this comprehensive collection compiled by one of America's most eminent folklorists. Here are tales of the West's prospectors, cowboys, bullwhackers, herders, homesteaders, lawmen, outlaws, judges, preachers, oilmen, hunters, rivermen, Indians, and Mormons, as well as such folk heroes as Billy the Kid, Wyatt Earp, Calamity Jane, Hugh Glass, and Buffalo Bill. Musical scores increase the usability of the songs and ballads. Author, title, and first line indexes of ballads and songs are included.

117 Dolch, Edward W. and Marguerite P.   *Tepee Stories*   (P, I)
in Basic Vocabulary.   Illus. by Robert S. Kerr.
Garrard, 1956.   165p.

The People lived by the Big River for many years. They made many houses of the Buffalo hides. They prayed to Mother Moon who had given them the Buffalo. And every year they went to Buffalo Hill and danced the Buffalo Dance.

This collection of folktales from the Pawnee, Blackfoot, Cheyenne, Wichita, Kiowa, Crow, Arikara, and Sioux Indians was written with the Dolch 220 Basic Sight Words. Included are stories of the creation of the world, the coming of the buffalo, and why Indians painted their bodies before going to war.

118 Federal Writers' Project, South Dakota. *Legends of*   (I)
the Mighty Sioux.   Illus. by Sioux Indian artists.   op
South Dakota Dept. of Public Instruction, 1941.
158p.   (Reprint ed., AMS Pr., 1975)

> Paha Sapa, or the Black Hills, have long been regarded by the Sioux as their holy land. Each year tribes came from great distances to cure illnesses in the warm springs and to hunt wild animals.

These forty-five authentic legends of places, mountains, battles, hunts, foods, dances, and songs were collected around the campfires and in interviews with the grandfather chiefs. Pupils in rural elementary schools suggested the pictures, which were redrawn by Oscar Howe, noted Indian artist. The preface describes the history and customs of the Sioux.

119 Marriott, Alice, and Rachlin, Carol K.   *Plains Indian*   (I, J)
Mythology.   Crowell, 1975.   194p.   (Paperback ed.,
New American Library, 1977)

> Tribal roots still are set deep in the soil that has been plowed, eroded, and in some places almost destroyed.

Presented as a continuum, myths, legends, and folklore of the Plains Indians are arranged in four parts—The Beginnings, The Little Stories: How and Why, Horseback Days, and Freedom's Ending. In an introduction to each tale the tribal origin is discussed and significant aspects are identified. An introduction to the people of the Plains and an epilogue concerning the Plains Indians today enhance its usefulness. Black-and-white photos of relevant museum pieces are included. An impressive bibliography indicating careful research is appended.

120 Pound, Louise. *Nebraska Folklore.*   Univ. of   (J, S)
Chicago Pr., 1913.   243p.   (Reprint ed., Greenwood   op
Pr., 1976)

> The customs to be recorded here are from the nineteenth century, though most persist into the twentieth and are, indeed, familiar to the majority of us today.

Compiled by one of the state's most distinguished writers, this volume contains folklore on a variety of subjects characteristic of Nebraska. Of particular interest is the chapter on "John G. Maher hoaxes" which outlines his life and reveals the variety of hoaxes he helped to perpetrate, among them the petrified man discovered near Chadron, the Alkali Lake Monster reputed to destroy cornfields and swallow a dozen calves at once, and the supposed discovery of the man who sunk the *Maine.* Animal and weather lore, folk customs, reports of cowboy songs, and famous people who gained legendary stature add depth to this unique work. An appendix provides helpful information on the study of folklore, dialect, and the American folk song. The lack of an index is unfortunate.

121 Sackett, S. J., and Koch, William E. *Kansas Folklore.*   (I, J, S)
     Univ. of Nebraska Pr., 1961. 251p.   op
     There is a great quantity of lore identifiably Kansan.

Many of the stories and tales in this collection deal with the trials of the early settlers. Even though they were harassed by Indians, duped by land speculators, and routinely plagued by illness, droughts, tornadoes, and insects, they faced their adversities with humor, song, and wit. Folk songs and ballads, dances and games, recipes, and superstitions make this anthology unique.

122 Welsch, Roger. *Shingling the Fog and Other Plains*   (J, S)
     Lies. Swallow, 1971. 160p.
     Times were so hard that the jack rabbits had to carry their own lunch.

Many people believe that the rigors of frontier life left little time for storytelling, singing, and cultural interchange. This collection discounts that belief. The weather, the land, big men, and strange critters, key elements in the pioneer's struggles for survival, were popular talltale subjects. A contest to choose the champion liar of Nebraska provided the motivation for some of the yarns. Others came from Kansas sources.

123 Welsch, Roger L., comp. *A Treasury of Nebraska*   (J, S)
     Pioneer Folklore. Univ. of Nebraska Pr., 1967. 391p.
     An empty wagon makes the most noise.

The folklore comprising this interesting volume consists of proverbs, songs, jokes, dances, customs, and much more. The two criteria for inclusion, interest and appeal, are evidenced throughout, from the familiar "Bury Me Not on the Lone Prairie" to the more elusive tale of "How Gold Came to the Black Hills." Recipes for "Poverty Cake," the directions for the children's game "Green Gravel," and the words for "Honey Comb Reel" are among the valuable tidbits of information available in this compendium of folklore.

POETRY, DRAMA, MUSIC

124 Benét, Stephen Vincent. *John Brown's Body.* Holt,   (S)
     1927. 336p. (Text ed., 1969)   op

I had . . . vainly flattered myself that without very much bloodshed, it might be done.

Henry Seidel Canby's introduction to the original edition says that the Benét poem is "beautiful as well as intricate . . . as realistic as it is romantic." Actual historical events of the Civil War form the backdrop against which the poem's characters, real and fictional, from both the North and the South, were developed and interpreted. The poem, awarded the Pulitzer Prize in 1929, is excellent for reader's theater adaptation.

125 Clark, Badger. *Sun and Saddle Leather: A Collection* (I, J, S)
of Poems. Chapman, 1915. 201p. (Reprint ed., op
Westerner's Foundation, 1962)

> I don't want no harps nor haloes
>> Robes nor other dressed up things—
> Let me ride the starry ranges
>> On a pinto hawse with wings.

Badger Clark, poet laureate of South Dakota, lived among cowboys most of his life. His poetry expressed his love for the prairie, its folklore, and its people. Earlier generations of South Dakota school children memorized "The Legend of Boastful Bill" and "A Cowboy's Prayer" and felt a kinship with the poet in his stiff-brimmed Stetson, flowing black tie, riding breeches, and boots.

126 Cleary, Kate McPhelim. *The Nebraska of Kate* (J, S)
McPhelim Cleary. United Educators, 1958. 238p. op

> When you get in one of those comfortable chairs . . . the Nebraska prairie seem[s] very far away.

The security of home is evidenced in the author's short stories and poetry. Each selection reveals an aspect of Nebraska life. Some, such as "Hired Girls," contain a wry humor, while others portray stark reality. In "On the Way West" a pioneer father and mother pause in their journey to bury their baby. All the selections appeal to the reader's emotions.

127 Cutler, Bruce. *A West Wind Rises.* Univ. of (S)
Nebraska Pr., 1962. 105p. op

> A Free State man said, "Gentlemen, if you intend to shoot, then take good aim."

The shocking Marais des Cygnes Massacre of 1858 has been vividly recorded in poetry such as the "Dispatch to the New York Tribune" and "Hanging of William Griffith." The suffering of the wives and mothers is poignantly expressed in "The Marriage of Lily Stillwell" and "Miriam Nickell's Letter to Her Mother." A study of historical events of this period will be greatly enhanced with the use of Cutler's poetry. A reader's theater adaptation would be particularly effective.

128 Foley, James W. *Foley's Poems.* Bismarck Tribune, (P, I, J, S)
nd. 223p.

There's a wholesomeness about it that I couldn't quite explain;
Once you breathe the air you love it and you long for it again.

The above lines are taken from Foley's best known poem, "A Letter Home." North Dakota's poet laureate visualizes for us the prairie life in the early days of the unspoiled West. Many of his poems are written in a folksy, homespun style.

129 Garson, Eugenia, comp. *Laura Ingalls Wilder*   (I, J, S)
Songbook: Favorite Songs from the "Little House"
Books. Illus. by Garth Williams. Harper, 1968.
160p.

In hard times or good there had always been Pa's songs and the voice of the fiddle, echoing longest of all.

Here are collected all the songs that appeared in the *Little House* books. The variety of types, including folk songs; old hymns and gospel songs; ballads, games, and dances; patriotic songs; and love songs, is enhanced by information about the songs, their composers, and lyricists. Each song is preceded by a quotation from the book in which it is mentioned. What fun for *Little House* devotees to sing as Laura and her family sang! A title and first line index are included.

130 Jaffe, Dan. *Dan Freeman.* Illus. by Aaron G. Pyle.   (S)
Univ. of Nebraska Pr., 1967. 73p. (Paperback ed.)

Let the mind feather the bird and it will fly.

Dan Freeman not only harbored soaring dreams, but also maintained a firm basis in the reality of pioneer Nebraska. As the first legal homesteader in the Nebraska Territory under the Homestead Act, he was active in the area's development. Not one to relinquish ideas for the sake of harmony, Freeman led a legal battle against religion in schools. Although his stand was unpopular, he won because his ideas were firmly grounded in the law. Jaffe blends his poetry with the events in Freeman's intriguing but stormy life to present a unique and sensitive view of a complex person.

131 Kliewer, Warren, and Solomon, Stanley J., eds.   (S)
Kansas Renaissance. Coronado Publications, 1961.   op
173p.

Authentic creative impulse is alive, . . . imaginations are at work.

Alan Crafton introduces the Kansan as writer in this collection of literary works prepared during the Kansas Centennial year. Poetry, a novelette, short stories, and plays by twenty-two outstanding Kansas authors are included, among them Kirke Mechem, Langston Hughes, and William Inge. Themes are generally universal rather than specifically relating to Kansas. W. R. Moses' poem "Big Dam" originated from opposition of farmers to the Tuttle Creek Dam project near Manhattan, Kansas, during the 1950s. The feeling expressed could be that of any farmer whose land was being confiscated.

132   Milton, John R., ed.   *The Literature of South Dakota.*   (S)
      Univ. of South Dakota Pr., 1976.   395p.

> It is my hope that the book may be read as a continuing story of South Dakota, a portrait from the time of Lewis and Clark to the present.

The author, professor of English at the University of South Dakota and editor of the literary magazine *South Dakota Review*, has compiled a chronological collection of works done by visitors, passers-through, and native writers. Included are excerpts from journals of exploration (*The Journals of Lewis and Clark*), travel narratives (Catlin's *Up the Missouri by Steamboat*), personal accounts of early settlement and homesteading (Garland's *Among the Corn Rows*), Indian folklore (McLaughlin's *Myths of the Sioux*), poetry (poems by Badger Clark and several contemporary poets), and works with Indian cultural themes (Black Elk's "Red Is the Knowledge"). Forty authors are represented, each with a brief biographical sketch.

133   Neihardt, John G.   *A Cycle of the West.*   5 vols.   (S)
      Macmillan, 1949.   656p.   (Paperback ed., Univ. of
      Nebraska Pr., 1971, under titles *The Twilight of the
      Sioux* and *The Mountain Men*)

> I had my village and my pony herds
> On Powder where the land was all my own.
> I wanted only to be let alone.

Neihardt's purpose in his writings was to preserve the courageous exploits of the period from 1822 to 1890, which he considered the epic period of American history. Here the explorers, fur traders, buffalo hunters, and Indian fighters are all treated with vigor and respect. Five narrative poems—"The Song of Hugh Glass" (1915), "The Song of Three Friends" (1919), "The Song of the Indian Wars" (1925), "The Song of the Messiah" (1935), and "The Song of Jed Smith" (1941)—constitute this work.

44

BIOGRAPHY AND PERSONAL ACCOUNTS

134 Adams, Alexander B. *Sitting Bull: An Epic of the*   (S)
         Plains. Putnam, 1973. 446p. (Paperback ed., 1974)

It is a book about Americans, Americans of all kinds and of types that are alive today.

This biography of the chief who defeated Custer is also a history of the Sioux Indian culture and the Plains Indian wars, which should help students understand the background of contemporary Indian problems. The author's sympathy is with Sitting Bull, who was determined to save the land of the buffalo for his people and their children. In spite of the book's orientation, the author implies that the wave of Western expansion was inevitable. Photographs, a section of narrative comments about the bibliographic sources, and an index accompany the text.

135 Alexander, Lloyd. *Border Hawk: August Bondi.*   (I, J)
         Illus. by Bernard Krigstein. Farrar, 1948. 182p.

But let the hand that tills the soil
Be like the wind that fans it: free!

August Bondi, a Viennese Jew, came to the United States with his parents as a young man. Working with John Brown, he became involved in the Kansas border disputes. After Brown's hanging, Bondi continued to champion the cause. During the Civil War Bondi served with Company K, Fifth Regiment, Kansas Volunteer Cavalry, and was severely wounded. After the war he became a respected Salina citizen and recorded the autobiography on which this book was based.

136 Anderson, Anita M., and Regli, Adolph. *Alec Majors.*   (P, I)
         Illus. by Jack Merryweather. (The American   op
         Adventure Series) Wheeler, 1953. 203p.

I will be on the trail as long as army forts are needed in the West.

Alexander Majors was a farm boy who grew up near Independence, Missouri. The Santa Fe Trail passed near his home, and he and his foster brother Charlie liked to watch the Conestoga wagons. In later years they traveled the trail many times themselves. Because of his high standards Alec became one of the most famous of the trail bosses. This easily-read biography vividly portrays the rigors of the trail.

137 Anderson, Lavere. *Sitting Bull: Great Sioux Chief.*   (P, I)
         Illus. by Cary. (Indian Books) Garrard, 1970. 80p.
         (Paperback ed., Dell, 1972)

He must be brave. He must be strong. . . . He must be generous.
He must be wise. These were the four Sioux virtues.

Writing about Indian/white relationships on the elementary level
without oversimplification or sentimentality is difficult. However, the
author succeeds in presenting Sitting Bull realistically from the time of
his boyhood escape from a grizzly until his death on Standing Rock
Reservation. Strong, brave, generous, and wise, even in defeat, he
proudly helped his people preserve their heritage. The orange and gold-
toned illustrations add a warm aura complementary to the text. A map
pinpointing locations of five important events in Sitting Bull's life is
included.

138   Aulaire, Ingri d' and Edgar Parin d'. *Buffalo Bill.*   (P, I)
      Doubleday, 1952. unp.
      Bill grew up at the edge of the plains, in the wilds of Kansas Ter-
      ritory.

Bill Cody's early playmates were Kickapoo Indian children. Kit
Carson and Wild Bill Hickok admired his roping and riding abilities.
Not only did he see the frontier develop from buffalo range to home-
steads, he also participated in the Indian wars precipitated by this
change. In later years his famous Wild West Show toured the United
States and Europe. The authors camped along Cody trails to gather material for this appealing biography which they illustrated.

139   Beckhard, Arthur J. *The Story of Dwight D.*   (J, S)
      Eisenhower. Illus. by Charles Geer. (Signature Books)   op
      Grosset, 1956. 180p.
      They were one of the busiest, happiest families in Abilene.

Dwight D. Eisenhower and his six brothers grew up in a close-
knit, loving family in Abilene, Kansas. Although the family was poor in
material wealth and Dwight sometimes even had to wear his mother's
shoes to school, they were rich in other ways. All the boys worked at
various jobs while assisting at home as well. They aided each other in
earning money for college. Eisenhower graduated from West Point and
was elected President of the United States after a military career.

140   Black Elk, Oglala Indian. *Black Elk Speaks; Being the*   (S)
      Life Story of a Holy Man of the Oglala Sioux, as told to   op
      John G. Neihardt (Flaming Rainbow). Illus. by
      Standing Bear. Morrow, 1932. 280p. (Paperback ed.,
      Pocket Books, 1972)
      A mighty vision given to a man too weak to use it.

In May 1931, John Neihardt visited Black Elk, a holy man of the

Sioux, in his log cabin home near Manderson, South Dakota. With his daughter as secretary, he faithfully recorded the old man's story. In Neihardt's words, "It was like half seeing, half sensing a strange and beautiful landscape by brief flashes of short lightning." This simple, impressive tale of the Indian's boyhood and life, of General Custer, of his second cousin Crazy Horse, of the Messiah craze, and of Wounded Knee is told with sensitivity and dignity.

141 Blackorby, Edward C. *Prairie Rebel: The Public Life* (S)
of William Lemke. Univ. of Nebraska Pr., 1963. 339p. op

The Nonpartisan League had almost become his religion, and it was having an effect on his personality.

William Lemke, one of the leaders of the farm-protest movement, assisted in the formation of the Nonpartisan League and participated in the historic 1916 session of the North Dakota legislature. Lemke is remembered for his role in national politics and his struggle on behalf of the two Frazier-Lemke bankruptcy acts.

142 Brown, Marion Marsh, and Crone, Ruth. *Willa Cather:* (J, S)
The Woman and Her Works. Scribner, 1970. 160p.

Willa . . . had found her "own quiet center of life," the life of the Nebraska plains.

From this "quiet center of life" came some of Willa Sibert Cather's best writing, writing which underscored the part played by immigrant settlers in Nebraska. She puzzled many people, for with some she was warm and human, with others, cold and imperious. Both moods earned her enemies and friends and caused many biographers to attempt to unravel her complex personality. Although Brown and Crone do not pretend to know what Willa was thinking in private moments, they speak as observers, relating events of Cather's life and her reactions to them. Documented with excerpts from her books and statements of others about her personality, the book's intriguing style challenges readers to draw their own conclusions about her. A list of suggested readings and an index are included.

143 Chandler, Edna Walker, and Willoughby, Barrett. (I)
Pioneer of Alaska Skies: The Story of Ben Eielson. Illus.
by Ray Quigley. Ginn, 1959. 179p.

At last he was soaring into the clouds, free as the wild geese he used to watch and envy.

In spite of his father's disapproval of flying, Carl Ben Eielson, who lived in Hatton, North Dakota, longed to fly, hoping someday to travel to Alaska. Returning home after basic aviation training in the army air service, he organized the Aero Club of Hatton. Later, while teaching school in Fairbanks, he worked on his plan for air transportation in Alaska.

144 Chrisman, Berna Hunter. *When You and I Were*   (J, S)
        Young, Nebraska! Purcell's, 1971. 255p.   op

We "grazed off the land" as much as possible.

The reader seeking one book containing both a factual account of the homesteader's life and a vigorous human element will be delighted with Berna Chrisman's account of her childhood and teen years in Nebraska. Although a number of other books deal with the homesteader's lot, this work details the homesteader's daily routine. The children's wild pets, their friends, and their love of music are described with sensitivity and humor. A short index is included.

145 Clark, Rose B. *My Nebraska Childhood: The Ought-*   (I, J, S)
        to-Biography of an Octogenarian.   Nebraska
        Wesleyan Pr., 1963. 68p.

In pioneer Nebraska, neighborliness was at its festive best when work was to be done.

House-raisings, huskings, and threshings were only a few of the aspects of life in the early days of Nebraska statehood which the author portrays in amusing, human style. The descriptions of her family, schooling, Friday afternoon programs, the local military band, and the family doctor are done with affection and attention to detail. Written from the viewpoint of the little girl who experienced these events, the book brings back a peaceful time, complete with homey descriptions. While the brevity of the account and the lack of plot may discourage some readers, others may appreciate the historic incidents not presented elsewhere.

146 Cook, Harold J. *Tales of the 04 Ranch.*   Univ. of   (J, S)
        Nebraska Pr., 1968. 221p.

I had trapped muskrats from the time I was very young, but as I grew older and could set larger traps, father taught me how to trap coyotes.

Writing in a conversational, first person style, Harold Cook recalls his boyhood on his father's ranch near the Niobrara River in northwestern Nebraska in the late 1800s. Breaking mustangs and broncs, braving blizzards, and maintaining peace with the Indians were all challenges to be faced. Taught by his father, a famous breeder of horses, Harold soon became skilled in a variety of ranch chores. While rigors and hardships were typical, daily life was not without humor, such as the time a skunk wandered into the cupboard and Father had to invent a way to coax it out. One exciting discovery was that 04, or Agate Springs Ranch, housed untouched fossil beds which Harold helped uncover. This interest in geology and paleontology gradually led Harold to attend the University of Nebraska to continue research and study.

147 Coombs, Charles. *Alaska Bush Pilot.* Illus. by   (I)
Raymon Naylor. Harper, 1963. 256p.   op

> "I came here to teach school," he said, "but what I really want to do is fly! Alaska needs aviation."

Based on the life of Carl Ben Eielson, this biography traces Eielson's life as an aviator from his determined struggle in completing flight training to his numerous efforts to prove that the airplane could solve Alaska's transportation problems. Although this book is not as readable as Chandler's *Pioneer of Alaska Skies*, this selection will appeal to students because it points up Eielson's courage and conviction.

148 Custer, Elizabeth B. *"Boots and Saddles"; or, Life*   (S)
in Dakota with General Custer. Harper, 1885. 312p.   op
(Reprint ed., Univ. of Oklahoma Pr., 1961)
(Paperback ed., Univ. of Oklahoma Pr., 1974; Berkshire
Traveller, 1977)

> Small misfortunes over which we amused ourselves.

Used to characterize problems encountered by the general's cook, the descriptive quotation could also describe the content of the book itself. Army life is composed of a myriad of small incidents which often assume disproportionate importance as they break the boredom and routine. These, not official matters, are the mainstays of this work. It does not gloss over the fear and worry when the men were in the field against the hostile Indians. It is, however, very laudatory of Custer. Mrs. Custer spent her life upholding the reputation of her husband, so diminished by death and defeat.

149 Custer, George Armstrong. *My Life on the Plains,*   (S)
or, Personal Experiences with Indians. Univ. of
Oklahoma Pr., 1962. 418p. (Paperback ed., Univ. of
Nebraska Pr., 1966; Citadel, 1974; Nordon Pr., 1976)

> There are two classes . . . who are always eager to get up an Indian war—the army and our frontiersmen.

The descriptive quotation, which Custer attempts unsuccessfully to refute, is from an Eastern newspaper. In fact, the entire book is a rebuttal of press coverage of prior events in his life and first appeared in serialized form in *The Galaxy,* a magazine of the day. A complete index follows the text.

150   DeLeeuw, Adele. *The Story of Amelia Earhart.*   (I, J)
      Illus. by Harry Beckoff. (Signature Books)   Grosset,   op
      1955. 181p.
      Women must try to do things as men have tried.

This account of Kansan Amelia Earhart highlights her adult years and her flying accomplishments in a field previously open only to men. Her exciting trip as the first woman to fly the Atlantic as a passenger prefaced her own solo Atlantic flight, the feat which brought her worldwide fame and honors. Her final flight with Fred Noonan is also recorded.

151   Dines, Glen. *Crazy Horse.* (A See and Read   (P)
      Beginning to Read Biography)   Putnam, 1966.   60p.   op
      "It is a good day to fight," he sang. "Brave hearts to the front."

It is difficult at the primary level to be accurate in detailing the lives of another era's heroes. The author in his sparse text (an average of five lines per page) and brown-toned illustrations succeeds well in catching the spirit and life of the great Sioux warrior. The book includes a list of key words.

152   Dresden, Donald. *The Marquis de Morès: Emperor*   (S)
      of the Bad Lands.   Univ. of Oklahoma Pr., 1970.
      282p. (Paperback ed., 1970)
      The air in Little Missouri and Medora crackled with protests over the fencing.

The cattle operations of the Marquis de Morès, who intended to supply eastern markets with range beef, were ill fated. His enterprise met the powerful opposition of the meat packers and the hostility of his North Dakota neighbors. The depth of the author's research is at times doubtful, and the organization of material makes the story somewhat difficult to follow. However, the book is useful in depicting the North Dakota range country of the 1880s.

153   Eastman, Charles A. *Indian Boyhood.* Illus. by E.L.   (J, S)
      Blumenschein. McClure, 1902. 289p. (Paperback   op
      ed., Dover, 1971)
      The Indian boy assumed the task of preserving . . . the legends of his ancestors.

The autobiography of Eastman's boyhood is the vehicle for preserving the legends of the Sioux and recording their way of life. The traditions, training of the young Indians, feasts and festivities, nomadic existence, and tribal government which prevailed in the era when the buffalo were still plentiful are vividly described.

154 Edwards, Leta M. *Sauce for the Geese: The Story of* (J, S)
a *Nebraska Farm.* Exposition, 1949. 125p. op

"Girls, G-i-r-l-s-s." Thus Mother broke the quiet of Monday morning.

Writing with an affectionate honesty, the author tells of her child-hood on a Nebraska dairy farm where she was the protesting partici-pant in the long hours of household, barnyard, and yard chores su-pervised by her mother. The father's brusque assessment of most situa-tions produces a mixture of consternation and humor in the story. Be-ginning when the author is approximately nine years old, the story traces her life until her graduation from business college at the age of eighteen. While the setting is one of the past, the family relationship is an enjoyable and familiar one. *Holi-daze on the Farm* (Exposition, 1952) continues the tale.

155 Farnsworth, Frances Joyce. *Winged Moccasins:* (J)
The Story of Sacajawea. Illus. by Lorence F.
Bjorklund. Messner, 1954. 189p.

Every time I climb a new hilltop I hold my breath for what I may see beyond.

Based on research conducted by two independent investigators, this biography of the Shoshone Indian woman who served as guide and interpreter for the famous Lewis and Clark expedition reveals Indian cus-toms as it recounts proven facts of her life. This historically accurate and sympathetic work also includes facts about her later years. Saca-jawea's desire to know what lay beyond the hilltops "where the geese flew and the streams flowed" appeals to the reader's spirit of adven-ture. Included are a bibliography of sources and an index.

156 Felton, Harold W. *Nat Love, Negro Cowboy.* Illus. (I)
by David Hodges. Dodd, 1969. 93p. op

The horse, with nostrils flared and flesh trembling with rage, reared but Nat stuck on his back.

Nat, a black slave born in Tennessee in 1854, set out for Kansas at the age of fifteen to become a cowboy. His life was full of adventure and excitement on the western cattle range. The episodes in this book are based upon Nat's autobiography, written in 1907, *The Life and Adventures of Nat Love: Better Known in the Cattle Country as "Dead-wood Dick."* He acquired this nickname at the Fourth of July celebration in Deadwood, South Dakota, in 1876, when he won both the shooting and the wild bronco roping and riding contests.

157   Fielder, Mildred.   *Wild Bill and Deadwood.*   (S)
Superior Publishing, 1965.   160p.   op

> He has been a legend in America's frontier since he was a young man. He remains a western legend today.

This well-researched biography by a native of the Black Hills is an attempt to separate fact from fiction and legend from reality. References at the close of each chapter, as well as an extensive bibliography, include primary sources. The text is illustrated with rare photos, many from state historical societies, universities, and museums. Although the quality of the photos varies, the effect is that of a well-captioned picture album of Hickok and Deadwood lore.

158   Filley, H. Clyde.   *Every Day Was New: The Story*   (S)
of the Growth of Nebraska.   Exposition, 1950.   179p.   op

> My schoolwork was easy, so I had time to listen to the older pupils recite.

That Nebraska's growth depended on the tenacity and resourcefulness of its pioneers is evidenced in this work. The events of the author's life parallel the development of Nebraska's industry, agriculture, and politics. Special emphasis is given to education because of the author's long career as a teacher and school administrator. Historic facts are laced with reminiscences of family and friends. While the style is less conversational than that of many autobiographies, older readers will gain a picture of Nebraska's role in the disturbed world of the depression period.

159   Franchere, Ruth.   *Willa: The Story of Willa Cather's*   (I, J)
Growing Up.   Illus. by Leonard Weisgard.   Crowell,
1958.   169p.

> There are so many interesting things to be! I want to be everything and read everything and see everything.

Propelled by limitless energy and a special form of curiosity, Willa hurtled through her childhood on the Nebraska prairie, doing her best to experience everything. The story of her life until she leaves home at sixteen to attend college gives insight into events and characters featured in her own later works. A brief bibliography is included.

160   Frazier, Neta Lohnes.   *Sacajawea: The Girl Nobody*   (J)
Knows.   McKay, 1967.   182p.   op

The Indian woman with us examined the moccasins which we found. . . . She says that her nation made their moccasins differently.

Excerpts from diaries of Lewis, Clark, and others who participated in the famous expedition are the basis for this work. The author is forced to conjecture about aspects of Sacajawea's life for which details are obscure. The work suggests her importance as an influential force in western settlement.

161 Garland, Hamlin. *A Son of the Middle Border.*   (S)
Illus. by Alice Barber Stephens. Macmillan, 1917.   op
467p. (Reprint ed., 1962)

> With that marvelous faith which marks the husbandmen, we went forth once more with the drill and the harrow, planting seed against another harvest.

Pulitzer Prize-winner Hamlin Garland records the contagious enthusiasm and holiday spirit of the settlers moving into the Dakotas as they view the deep rich soil with promise. In dramatic contrast is their later, bitter acceptance of monotony, unremitting toil, desperate fatigue, and disillusionment. This autobiography serves well as an antidote to the romanticism often associated with frontier living.

162 Garst, Shannon. *Crazy Horse, Great Warrior of the*   (I, J)
Sioux. Illus. by William Moyers. Houghton, 1950.
260p.

> Leadership is a gift from the *Wakan Tanka.* To be used for the good of the people.

From his youth Has-ka, the light-skinned one, dreamed of being a leader with a manly name. When he earned the name Crazy Horse, signifying an untamed, splendid horse of great courage, he achieved part of his goal. At the completion of his vision quest, he realized that he had been set apart by the Great Holy Mystery for greatness. This fictionized biography of the Sioux leader who fought against the invasion of the whites is often brutal, often blood-soaked, but it is also full of sensitivity for the Indian leader and his people. A chronology of his life and a bibliography are useful features.

163 Garst, Shannon. *Sitting Bull: Champion of His*   (J)
People. Illus. by Elton C. Fax. Messner, 1946. 189p.

> Where are our lands? Who stole them? Who slew our warriors and our women and children?

To hold back the flood of white civilization, this Dakota chief fought long and valiantly. Wanting neither gifts of money nor war, he only desired freedom for his people to hunt, fish, and dance on Indian hunting grounds without the white man's encroachment. Yet the white man's treaties proved to be worthless, and the good way of life for the Indians came to an end. This fictional biography includes a chronology of Sitting Bull's life, a bibliography, and a complete index.

164 Garst, Shannon and Warren. *Wild Bill Hickok.*   (J, S)
Messner, 1952. 183p.   op

> Whatever it is inside me that pushes me, tells me that it's my duty to bring peace and law and order to the plains.

When he was twelve years old, Hickok solemnly promised his mother that he would always be on the side of law and right. However, she worried about him because he was the most handsome man she had ever seen, and he craved excitement. This is a thrill-packed biography of a hero whose bullets spoke for frontier justice in times of the Civil War, Indian uprisings, and outlaw raids. His greatest love was America itself. A chronology, bibliography, and index are included.

165 Geelan, Agnes. *The Dakota Maverick: The Political*   (S)
Life of William Langer, Also Known as "Wild Bill"
Langer. Kaye's Printing, 1976. 166p.

> Bill Langer came to the United States Senate well-qualified as a maverick.

Since William Langer had been a maverick in state politics, it is no surprise that he continued in the same pattern by bolting the Republican party to vote with the Democrats thirty-seven out of sixty times in 1947. He delayed the confirmation of Supreme Court Justice Warren, and his was one of two Republican votes which blocked confirmation of a cabinet member. The author seems to admire Langer's political acumen, although she scrupulously describes his flamboyant love of power, his questionable activities, and the poor national impression he frequently made.

166 Glad, Paul W. *The Trumpet Soundeth: William*   (S)
Jennings Bryan and His Democracy, 1896–1912.   op
Univ. of Nebraska Pr., 1960. 242p. (Paperback ed.,
1966)

> The "ism" he became was fashioned with forceful affection by the rural society in which he lived and moved and had his being.

Glad begins by presenting the influences of Protestantism, *McGuffey's Readers,* and the Chautauqua in shaping Bryan's later activities and in so doing reveals patterns of culture that shaped many lives in the midwest. Through his stand on reforms relating to tariffs, trusts, and the regulation of business, Bryan is portrayed as a heroic figure whose political influence was lasting. Extensive notes and a bibliographical essay contribute to this scholarly, readable work.

167   Governor's Commission on the Status of Women.   (I, J, S)
       Nebraska Women through the Years, 1867–1967.   op
       Johnsen Publishing, 1967.   72p.

> Nebraska's woman . . . owes much to . . . those who battled for these things she enjoys today.

Medicine, education, and sociology are only a few of the fields of endeavor to which Great Plains women have made significant contributions. The life of the Indian woman is detailed in these pages, especially the contributions of the La Flesche women, members of one of the first families to realize the necessity for peaceful coexistence between Indians and whites. Though the treatment of its subjects is brief, this slim booklet gives a compact overview absent from many history volumes. Exceptional in its discussion of the roles of women outside the home, this book fills an important void.

168   Green, Norma Kidd.   *Iron Eye's Family: The Children*   (S)
       of Joseph La Flesche.   Johnsen Publishing, 1969.
       225p.

> Few other families of the generation that was forced to find a way to new values have as many outstanding figures.

Joseph La Flesche, or Iron Eye, was the last man to become chief of the Omaha tribe through participation in the age-old rituals. The story about him and his family is one of achievement in the white man's world, for the La Flesches kept their hearts in tune with tribal problems and did not remove themselves completely from the geographical setting of their old culture. In this carefully documented family account, the history of the Omaha Indians in Nebraska comes to life.

169   Harrington, Lyn.   *The Luck of the La Vérendryes.*   (I, J)
       Nelson, 1967.   157p.   op

> Someone had accomplished the La Vérendryes' quest at last.

Pierre de La Vérendrye was one of the last of the French-Canadian explorers. He and his sons worked together to establish forts and trading posts across the Northwest. The first whites to see the Badlands, the explorations of the La Vérendryes were accompanied by many adventures and hardships. Their dream finally was realized when Alexander Mackenzie reached the Pacific. The book's readable style is evidence of the author's enthusiasm for the subject.

170   Hatch, Alden. *Young Ike.*   Illus. by Jules Gotlieb.   (P, I)
Messner, 1953.   147p.   (Paperback ed., Archway, nd)

     The family bonds were so closely woven by work and happiness and troubles shared that they remained the strongest tie in the lives of all the brothers.

A loving, close-knit family is portrayed in this story of the boyhood of Dwight D. Eisenhower, thirty-fourth president of the United States. Growing up on a modest Kansas farm on the outskirts of Abilene, Ike and his five brothers did farmwork, housework, cooking, delivered newspapers, sold vegetables, worked at the creamery, and sandpapered animals for merry-go-rounds.

171   Haverstock, Mary Sayre. *Indian Gallery: The Story of*   (J, S)
George Catlin.   Four Winds Pr., 1973.   229p.

     To Catlin these were . . . real men and women, honorable, kind, good people who—unless white men changed their ways—were doomed to a lingering and cruel death.

Haverstock spent a summer retracing George Catlin's travels up the Missouri River. This experience, the inclusion of many quotations from Catlin's letters and journals, and reproductions of his artwork provide vitality and authenticity to her well-written biography. Also of value are Catlin's 1841 map showing the location of the tribes he visited and two diagrams detailing his travels from 1830 to 1836. Style, format, and thorough indexing make this book particularly useful for history, art, and background reading on contemporary Indian problems.

172   Herron, Edward A. *Wings over Alaska. The Story of*   (I, J)
Carl Ben Eielson.   Messner, 1959.   192p.   (Paperback
ed., Archway, nd)

     "She's on her way," he whispered, "I'm going to fly." Thus Ben Eielson assured himself that the long-awaited airplane was actually being shipped to Alaska.

Eielson, portrayed as an energetic, daring pilot, soared to fame as the pioneer hero who was the first to fly over the North Pole. His early years in Hatton, North Dakota, his army training, barnstorming, teaching, and struggle to establish Alaska's first commercial air service are presented in an informative, realistic manner. His life and lasting contribution provide a story of real adventure.

173   Hertzler, Arthur. *Horse and Buggy Doctor.*   R. West,   (S)
1938.   332p.   (Reprint ed., Univ. of Nebraska Pr.,   op
1970)   (Paperback ed., 1970)

     Your Kansan may fear God, but he fears neither man nor the devil.

The anecdotes and experiences of a country doctor who began practicing in Kansas before the turn of the century serve as a historical record and an interesting contrast to present-day medical practices. The struggles and growth of privately-owned hospitals are also described. Although the historical record is valuable, the appeal of the book is found in the colorful Dr. Hertzler himself.

174 Holbrook, Stewart H. *Wild Bill Hickok Tames the*   (I)
     West. Illus. by Ernest Richardson. (Landmark
     Books) Random, 1952. 179p.

> Can't you come here for a few days and put the fear of law and order into these cut-throats?

From the Underground Railroad experiences of his youth in Illinois until his assassination in Deadwood, Dakota Territory, James Butler Hickok's life was exciting. Until official law arrived, he tamed and quieted the border settlements. Pioneer Kansas towns (Leavenworth, Abilene, Fort Riley, Hays City) benefited from his fearlessness, his honesty, his courage—and his six-shooter. This easy-to-read, exciting biography has wide appeal.

175 Holbrook, Stewart H. *Wyatt Earp, U.S. Marshal.*   (I, J)
     Illus. by Ernest Richardson. (Landmark Books)   op
     Random, 1956. 180p.

> He was the first frontier peace officer who believed that peace could be enforced without bloodshed.

After successfully completing his term as lawman in Wichita, Wyatt Earp accepted Mayor George Hoover's offer of a similar job in Dodge City. Wyatt's brothers and Doc Holliday worked with him in Dodge City and later in Tombstone, Arizona, where Wyatt served as a United States marshal. Wyatt Earp died quietly in 1929 at eighty years of age without possessing a single bullet scar.

176 Howe, Jane Moore. *Amelia Earhart: Kansas Girl.*   (P, I)
     Illus. by Paul Laune. (Childhood of Famous
     Americans) Bobbs-Merrill, 1950. 196p.

> It's the most wonderful feeling in the world—up in the sky alone, flying through snowy clouds.

Amelia Earhart's childhood was spent in Atchison, Kansas, where she lived with her grandparents. As a young child, Amelia displayed the traits of independence and bravery which later distinguished her. She was honored by President Hoover for her solo trans-Atlantic flight in May 1932. Her simply told story is excellent for beginning biography readers.

177 Hutton, Harold. *Doc Middleton: Life and Legends*   (S)
of the Notorious Plains Outlaw. Swallow Pr., 1974.
290p.

He did nothing toward the advancement of civilization on the
frontier and probably regretted seeing settled society come.

Notorious Doc Middleton, known Nebraska rustler, took as his
motto "travel light, travel fast, travel friendly." His Robin Hood reputation is doubtful, however, as he admitted stealing horses from a man
who had cared for him one winter. He married three times, using
different aliases because he was wanted for murder. No one knows just
how many horses he and his gang rustled or how many people they
killed because he was blamed for many unlawful acts which he may not
have committed. Constructed from elusive records and family interviews, the book is documented with copious notes and a selected
bibliography.

178 Iger, Eve Marie. *John Brown: His Soul Goes*   (J, S)
Marching On. Young Scott, 1969. 159p.   op

Much of the roughness in John Brown's story is the roughness of the
frontier.

A visit to Harper's Ferry stimulated the author's interest in John
Brown and inspired her work. Early childhood events and experiences
during Brown's growing years are presented in an effort to account for
his actions at Harper's Ferry in 1859. Numerous illustrations, a well-
documented text, and careful indexing provide a valuable resource for
the pre-Civil War period in American history.

179 Johnson, Dorothy M. *Warrior for a Lost Nation:*   (I, J)
A Biography of Sitting Bull; with Sitting Bull's Own   op
Pictographs. Westminster, 1969. 173p.

A "sitting bull" was one that held his ground, that could not be
pushed aside.

An adopted member of the Blackfoot tribe, the author demonstrates her journalistic talents in this biography of the noted Dakota
warrior. Providing both the Indian and white viewpoints, the text gives
a balanced account of Sitting Bull's life from childhood to death, as well
as a description of the robbery of his grave in 1953. Many quotations
from contemporary sources and copies of fifteen pictographic drawings
by Sitting Bull add authenticity. A bibliography and index are provided.

180 Johnson, John R. *Representative Nebraskans.* Illus.   (J, S)
by Clarence E. Struble. Johnsen Publishing, 1954.
198p.

It takes all kinds of people to build a state. Nebraska has been built by farmers, ranchers, business and professional men . . . as well as politicians.

Nebraska has produced a widely diversified and highly talented group of individuals whose accomplishments have given them a special place in history. A wide range of activity is found, from the achievements of baseball star Grover Cleveland Alexander to the political ideals of George W. Norris. Included in this biography of thirty-five persons, most of whom are men, are social worker Grace Abbott, merchant Jonas L. Brandeis, telegraph pioneer Edward Creighton, Boys' Town founder Father Flanagan, and movie personalities Robert Taylor and Daryl Zanuck. The life of each person included is described in a detailed yet interesting manner. A bibliography is included.

181 Jones, Gene. *Where the Wind Blew Free: Tales of*   (J, S)
        Young Westerners. Norton, 1967. 195p.   op

> Westward, beyond the Mississippi, feel the space, hear the silence, touch the wind.

The author sympathetically presents ten little-known young men and women whose lives were part of the drama of the westward movement. Among those included are the stories of Baptiste Charbonneau, son of Sacagawea and a French trader; of Cynthia Ann Parker who, after twenty-four years as a Comanche captive, died of loneliness among her white relatives; and of Johnny Baker, foster son of Buffalo Bill Cody, who filmed a historical movie at the site of Wounded Knee. Each chapter is preceded by an introduction to provide historical perspective. An index increases the usefulness.

182 Karolevitz, Robert F. *"E.G.," Inventor by Necessity:*   (J, S)
        The Story of E. G. Melroe and the Melroe Company.   op
        North Plains Pr., 1968. 160p.

> Anything he bought at the hardware store or from an implement dealer, he'd have to change.

E. G. Melroe, Gwinner, North Dakota farmer, used ingenuity, perseverance, and hard work to improve farm equipment and develop a multimillion-dollar family enterprise. His inventive genius prevailed in spite of the loss of a leg, drought, depression, and financial difficulties. His family's flexibility and cohesiveness contributed to his success.

183 Karolevitz, Robert F. *Where Your Heart Is: The*   (S)
        Story of Harvey Dunn, Artist. North Plains Pr., 1970.
        207p.

> I prefer painting pictures of early South Dakota life to any other kind . . . my search for other horizons has led me around to my first.

The life of Harvey Dunn, born in a claim shanty near Manchester, South Dakota, is traced to the sophisticated art centers of the East and back again. Under the tutelage of Howard Pyle he became successful as an "artist in olive drab" who painted World War I from the civilian point of view. However, his greatest work was based on the simplicity and strength of the prairie scenes of his boyhood. Included among the book's many illustrations is his best-known "The Prairie is My Garden," a magnificent portrayal of the everlasting hope of a frontier wife. The Harvey Dunn Collection and Archives is on the campus of South Dakota State University at Brookings.

184 Kauffman, Bernice, comp. *Nebraska Centennial*   (I, J, S)
Literary Map and Guide to Nebraska Authors.   op
Nebraska Centennial Commission, 1967. 62p.

> It is hoped that the Nebraska Centennial Literary Map and Guide to Nebraska Authors will stimulate the imagination of Nebraska's citizens.

Although brief and not always comprehensive, this booklet provides thumbnail sketches of the lives of authors who were either born in Nebraska or who wrote substantially about the state. The inclusion of the autobiography of Fred Astaire indicates that all of the entries are not necessarily authors in their own right; nonetheless, the booklet is a useful resource. A literary map showing the homes of many authors is a valuable visual aid. A bibliography of consulted sources is included.

185 Kelley, Peggy A. Volzke. *Women of Nebraska Hall*   (I, J, S)
of Fame. Illus. by Joan I. Tomlinson. Arbor
Printing, 1976. 112p.

> Womanhood is not a product of legislation and cannot be abolished by law.

This statement by Esther Carter Griswold-Warner, a pioneer Nebraska farmer and suffragist, provides the tone for this brief but detailed work. Far from being a women's liberation tract, the book provides a one-page outline of the lives of more than forty outstanding Nebraska women. Each biography is accompanied by a portrait; and women from such fields as education, agriculture, politics, art, literature, the social sciences, business, aviation, and journalism are represented. Source material is listed for researchers wishing to read more about a specific person.

186 King, James T. *War Eagle: A Life of General Eugene*   (S)
A. Carr. Univ. of Nebraska Pr., 1964. 321p.

> "What can equal the pleasure, for a man," he had asked, "of risking life, & hoping for fame, in upholding a cause he deems just."

From distinguished service in the Civil War, Carr returned to the frontier where he was a competent, successful officer, concerned about his men, and committed to serving the cause of westward expansion as he saw it. In the controversy over the bloody Battle of Cibicu Creek which forced his retirement, Carr is seen as a stubborn man, dissatisfied with a record implying any error in judgment on his part. Extensive notes document the work, and the list of primary sources evidences a scholarly approach. The book is useful in a full appraisal of a bitter chapter in American history.

187 Kosner, Alice. *The Voice of the People: William*   (J, S)
         Jennings Bryan. Messner, 1970. 190p.

   The first battle is over. But there will be others—and I shall continue to fight for what I believe in.

William Jennings Bryan's life was a series of battles from the schoolboy debates in which he discovered the powers of oratory to his frustration at the Scopes trial. His position on many political issues made him one of the most controversial figures of the late nineteenth and early twentieth centuries. The book begins with Bryan's birth in southern Illinois and traces his career until his death in 1925. The influence of his father on his religious beliefs, his ordinary upbringing, and the political events of the times are described in detail in a manner which helps the reader understand the personality of this controversial figure who considered Nebraska his home. A bibliography and index are included.

188 Kyner, James H. *End of Track.* Caxton, 1937.   (J, S)
         280p. (Paperback ed., Univ. of Nebraska Pr., 1960)   op

   "Now, remember," I went on . . . "if this money don't reach camp, it'll be because I'm dead!"

Jim Kyner's life exposed him to many dangerous adventures. After losing a leg at the Battle of Shiloh during the Civil War and trying his hand at homesteading and politics, he went westward with the railroad. Finding the challenging but precarious life to his liking, he became involved in the construction of railroads throughout the West. Many of Jim's jobs brought him to Nebraska, and through these experiences he conveyed the flavor of an area trying on its statehood for the first time. This account of one man who goes to new territory to escape the discouragement of the post-Civil War years typifies the story of many. A section of notes adding historical details follows this entertaining, informative narrative.

189 Levine, Lawrence W. *Defender of the Faith: William*   (S)
         Jennings Bryan, The Last Decade, 1915–1925. Oxford   op
         Univ. Pr., 1965. 386p. (Paperback ed., 1968)

If his final years ended in tragedy, it was not the tragedy of a good man gone bad, but the tragedy of a good faith too blindly held and too uncritically applied.

Concentrating on the last ten years of Bryan's life, Levine reveals that Bryan did not end his days transformed from radical to ultraconservative, as his critics were wont to believe. The convictions underlying Bryan's actions—the belief in majority rule, the faith in the sanctity of the Bible, and the championing of the rights of the agrarian population—influenced and dominated his entire career. This carefully documented work does much to dispel the image of a broken man dying five days after the end of the Scopes trial. It is a useful companion to Glad's *The Trumpet Soundeth* which deals with an earlier segment of Bryan's political career.

190   Lovelace, Delos W.   *"Ike" Eisenhower: Statesman*   (I, J)
           and Soldier of Peace.   Crowell, 1957.   279p.   (Rev.   op
           ed., 1969)

When ceremony and protocol seemed about to smother him he sometimes shrugged it off, insisting that he was "just a farm boy from Kansas."

Dwight D. Eisenhower's life is recounted from his boyhood to his presidential campaign. His years at West Point, marriage to Mamie Doud, and army career culminating in his rise to a post of supreme command in World War II receive authoritative treatment. His ability to return to peacetime jobs with the same skill and thoroughness that matched his wartime triumphs further reveals his character.

191   Lowitt, Richard.   *George W. Norris: The Making of a*   (S)
           Progressive, 1861–1912.   Syracuse Univ. Pr., 1963.
           341p.

Norris' remarks were seldom without purpose. . . . He seldom failed to inform his listeners.

This biography of George Norris, one of the most influential of Nebraska's leaders, traces his life from his boyhood on an Ohio farm through law school and young adulthood until his entrance into the U.S. Senate in 1913. His political growth and maturing are recounted, as is the parallel progress of the state of Nebraska, which he adopted early in his career. The story flows freely and details are related clearly and accurately. The text is illustrated with photographs and an occasional political cartoon. An index is included. The remainder of Norris's life is discussed in Lowitt's *George W. Norris: The Persistence of a Progressive, 1913–1933* (Univ. of Illinois Pr., 1971).

192 McKelvie, Martha. *Sandhills Essie.* Dorrance, 1964. (S)
  95p.   op

> "Compromise!" yelled Essie. "I have never compromised when I knew I was right!"

Life on a sandhills cattle ranch was precarious at best, but for widowed Essie Davis and her four-month-old son, a secure future seemed impossible. However, instead of selling the ranch to return to the millinery business, Essie endeavored to gain expertise at cattle raising. She succeeded and became one of Nebraska's most respected citizens. The biography does not follow a strict chronological sequence and defines Essie's personality and success through anecdotes.

193 Meadowcroft, Enid LaMonte. *Crazy Horse: Sioux* (P)
  Warrior. Illus. by Cary. (Indian Books) Garrard,
  1965. 80p.

> Today, my son has fought bravely against a strange tribe. . . . I give him the great name my father gave to me . . . Crazy Horse.

This narrative combines details of a typical Oglala boyhood when Crazy Horse was known as "Curly," continues through his emergence as a leader who fought to preserve the homeland of his people from the white soldiers, and ends with his stabbing in a jail at Fort Robinson. The Cary illustrations are outstanding. This action-filled, fictional biography will appeal to those children who like excitement and to those who need encouragement to read.

194 Meadowcroft, Enid LaMonte. *The Story of Crazy* (P, I)
  Horse. Illus. by William Reusswig. (Signature op
  Books) Grosset, 1954. 181p.

> If you are true to your wisdom and think often of the good of the people, you will someday be a leader.

From his carefree boyhood days along the Niobrara River to his tragic death in the white man's jail cell, Crazy Horse is presented as a great Native American who fought courageously for the freedom of his people. Red Cloud urged his brothers to drive the whites out before it was too late, but Chief Smoke believed they were friends with whom the Indians should keep peace. As a result, a treaty was signed at Fort Laramie guaranteeing gifts from the white men every year for fifty years in exchange for forts. This sympathetic treatment of Crazy Horse's life dramatically reveals the tragic consequences of the treaty's violation.

195 Mohberg, Nora. *The Straddlebug.* Record Printers, (J, S)
  1968. 261p.   op

"Be sure to put up a 'straddle bug' when you have made your choice of land," warned the surveyor's assistant.

Based on the author's early life, this is an excellent story of a Norwegian family who homesteaded in North Dakota. It pictures not only life on the prairie but also the political building of a country from territory to state, from settlement to thriving city. It should attract those who enjoy North Dakota history as well as those of Norwegian ancestry.

196 Neihardt, John G. *All Is but a Beginning.* Harcourt,   (J, S)
1972. 173p.

"Hold fast, hold fast; there is more!"

The message to young people in the quotation becomes a central theme of the author's account of his own youth. In eighty-two short episodes that took place from 1881 until the end of the century, he remembers the small events that later became lines in his poetic works. Among these recollections are the bell-ringing experiences that financed the college education which enabled him to teach in a rural school, as well as the search for a job in Kansas City and the fateful trip to work in flooded timber that was part of his youthful attempt to conquer the world. His first published work, *The Divine Enchantment*, though it ended in flames set by his own hand, marked the beginning of a successful writing career. This readable narrative is in itself a social history of the troubled times that characterized the late 1890s.

197 Nelson, Cordner. *The Jim Ryun Story.* Tafnews   (I, J, S)
Press, 1967. 272p.   op

I consider Jim's accomplishments off the track almost the equal of his world records.

On Sunday, July 17, 1966, a nineteen-year-old Wichita, Kansas, athlete ran the mile faster than any other person ever had before. Within twenty-four hours more than a billion people had heard the news. Jim Ryun's personal story is as important as his running achievements. As he constantly sought perfection in himself, he was also concerned with the feelings of others. He bore well the responsibilities that accompanied fame.

198 Nicoll, Bruce H., and Keller, Ken R. *Sam McKelvie:*   (J, S)
Son of the Soil. (Nebraska Heritage) Johnsen
Publishing, 1954. 174p.

The originally pleasant dream of someday being governor was . . . an obsession. . . . He must win the office.

Samuel Roy McKelvie managed to satisfy his political obsession after many years of disappointment. Influenced by his father who had had a no-nonsense attitude toward farm chores, McKelvie was not frightened by the prospect of hard work. Thus each setback he encountered was followed by renewed efforts to achieve his goal. The description of the political climate of Nebraska and the nation, coupled with the detailed characterization of Sam McKelvie, make this an appropriate choice for readers seeking historic facts with a personal flavor. Photographs of the McKelvies and of scenes from Nebraska's history are included.

199   Nolan, Jeannette Covert.   *John Brown.*   Illus. by   (I, J)
      Robert Burns.   Messner, 1950.   181p.

    I believe in the Declaration of Independence, the Golden Rule, race equality.

Employing the freedom of a novelist, the author presents a fascinating biography of "Old Brown of Kansas." Readers will find that many different interpretations of Brown's activities are available. Events recorded here portray Brown's belief that the Harper's Ferry incident was the ultimate goal of his life. The book will serve as excellent background for more advanced material on Brown.

200   Norris, George W.   *Fighting Liberal.*   Macmillan,   (S)
      1945.   419p.   (Paperback ed., 1961)   op

    The life of Norris is the story of America at its best.

Raised on an Ohio farm, Norris's formal education at Valparaiso Normal School was interrupted frequently because he had to quit school to raise money to continue. After graduation he taught in Whitehouse, Ohio, before moving to Nebraska. An avid Republican, he was soon elected district judge; and after serving seven years in this capacity, he began his career in the U.S. House of Representatives. Norris stood behind his beliefs and was instrumental in championing much-needed legislation. Among his more famous causes were establishing the TVA, advocating the Lame Duck Amendment, and supporting anti-injunction legislation. Known for his hard work and integrity, Norris, it is said, would not speak on any issue unless he had all the facts. This well-documented autobiography gives insight into the life of the famous congressman.

201   North, Luther.   *Man of the Plains: Recollections of*   (S)
      Luther North, 1856–1882.   (The Pioneer Heritage
      Series) Univ. of Nebraska Pr., 1961.   350p.

    This was the end of the organization of the Pawnee Indian scouts. They were true and loyal soldiers; brave as any body of men I ever saw.

In highly readable fashion the chronological story of Luther's life begins with his early youth on the Nebraska frontier. In service with the Pawnee Indian scouts, Captain North and his brother Frank played a vital role in the battle for control of the Great Plains. Later Luther formed a ranching partnership with Frank North and William F. Cody. The original manuscript was edited by Donald Danker with only minor changes to correct typing errors, establish chapter divisions, and supplement areas which appeared unclear. An appendix includes letters written by Luther North which are particularly pertinent or shed light on information in the main body of the work. A chronology of significant events in Great Plains history is a useful added resource.

202 O'Connell, Frank. *Farewell to the Farm.* Caxton, (S)
1962. 198p. op

If I have any children, they're going to get a good education.

Frank O'Connell's mother believed in education, and on this conviction she based her life. Raising a family of eleven children on a farm outside Lincoln, Nebraska, was neither easy nor glamorous, but education seemed the key to a successful future. O'Connell's story of his family's struggles for success is related with frankness and affection. The manner in which his family faces the problems of disease, prairie fire, crop failure, and drought in reaching its goals makes a highly readable story.

203 O'Connor, Richard. *Sitting Bull: War Chief of the* (I, J)
Sioux. Illus. by Eric von Schmidt. McGraw-Hill, op
1968. 144p.

Young men, help me . . . help me
I love my people so—
That is why I am fighting.

Sitting Bull was a poet, a diplomat, a warrior, a compassionate chief, and a reverent medicine man. This sympathetic, thought-provoking biography accents his desire to live at peace with white men on condition that they leave his people alone. He feared that peace would come, however, only when Indians walked the white man's road. He saw no reason for giving away the land that had always belonged to his people; and ultimately, for this conviction he gave his life.

204 Parks, Gordon. *A Choice of Weapons.* Harper, 1966. (J, S)
274p. (Paperback ed., 1973)

There was always something inside of this man which . . . he forced to flower and bear fruit.

Gordon Parks, the youngest of fifteen children in a poor farm family, spent his first sixteen years in Fort Scott, Kansas, where he was born. The underlying theme of this autobiographical sketch is the author's belief in his own potential. Anger and despair are evident, but a determination to succeed despite unfair treatment prevails. An investment in a used camera opened avenues to Parks that led to a successful career in photography.

205   Plate, Robert. *Palette and Tomahawk: The Story of*   (J, S)
         George Catlin, July 27, 1796–December 23, 1872.   op
         Illus. [adapted] from drawings by George Catlin.
         McKay, 1962. 248p.

> Takes a real feel for Indians to paint them as they are. Judging by your work, son, you can do it.

In his later years George Catlin rejoiced that he had been born at the right time to paint Indians in their native dignity, untouched, unspoiled, undefeated. To this end he had sacrificed a law career and a happy home life with his wife and family, but he produced a rich legacy of art. He faithfully and sympathetically portrayed the Indians and recorded scenes of animals, encampments, and prairie vistas. Line drawings give a hint of the originals for which he is famous. This inspiring fictional biography demonstrates one man's struggle to eliminate prejudice.

206   Raaen, Aagot. *Measure of My Days.*   North Dakota   (J, S)
         Institute for Regional Studies, 1953. 323p.

> Yes, one's conscience is a good guide.

For Aagot Raaen, daughter of Norwegian pioneers in North Dakota, successful struggles with blizzards, illnesses, and despondency gave her the willpower and perseverance to become a well-educated woman. She taught in one-room schools and later, as county superintendent of schools, fought for improved educational opportunities. Miss Raaen traveled to many foreign countries whose splendor intrigued her, but she always returned to North Dakota where her life was a lesson in the dignity of work. Her style of writing reflects the simplicity and directness of the Norwegian settlers in North Dakota.

207   Rockwell, Anne. *Paintbrush & Peacepipe: The Story*   (I)
         of George Catlin.   Atheneum, 1971. 86p.

> Slowly an idea began to form in Catlin's mind. . . . He would go West and visit the people of the Great Plains, paint portraits of them.

Through his paintings of the Indians of the Plains, George Catlin attempted to interpret Indian life to white people. Here are recorded in a straightforward, undramatic style events such as his first encounter, at the age of ten, with an Indian; his friendship with General William Clark, which culminated in his voyage up the Missouri on the *Yellowstone*; his attempts to establish a national Indian gallery; and his travels to Europe and South America. Unfortunately, the sinopia illustrations bear little resemblance to Catlin's work.

208   Rolfsrud, Erling Nicolai.   *Extraordinary North*   (I, J, S)
          Dakotans.   Lantern Books, 1954.   228p.   op
   With Dorothy and her husband playing the mother and father, "Life with Father" was produced on Broadway.

Dorothy Stickney was a North Dakotan who became a successful Broadway actress, playing leading parts not only in *Life with Father* but in other stage productions as well. The brief sketch about her is one of many included in Rolfsrud's work which provides difficult-to-find information about North Dakotans whose lives and accomplishments demonstrated an indomitable spirit.

209   Rolfsrud, Erling Nicolai.   *Lanterns over the*   (I, J)
          Prairies, books 1 & 2.   Lakeland Pr., 1949, 1950.   op
          160p., 146p.
   There are lanterns over the prairies still!

Today's lanterns shine from the lives of ordinary North Dakotans who lived extraordinary lives. The roster of those people described in the two volumes includes Indians, writers, agricultural researchers, farmers, and the "flower lady." The stories are designed to inspire pride in the pioneer heritage. An index is provided.

210   Russell, Don.   *The Lives and Legends of Buffalo Bill.*   (S)
          Univ. of Oklahoma Pr., 1960.   514p.
   Will [Cody] followed a rainbow trail all his life, but never quite caught up with the pot of gold.

Although Buffalo Bill's wanderings make it difficult to assign him a home state, Nebraska is where he chose to retire, having crossed it frequently during his days as a bullwhacker and buffalo hunter. Like all who have reached the stature of folk hero, the person often is overtaken by legend until it is difficult to separate the two. Drawing together several accounts of Buffalo Bill, Russell presents and compares them in a highly readable style. The author does not pick one "correct" account; many facts support the legends. The reader can conclude that any version of William F. Cody's life must be read critically. Footnotes, a bibliography, and an index are included.

211   Sandoz, Mari.   *Crazy Horse: The Strange Man of the*   (S)
          Oglalas.   Hastings, 1942.   424p.   (Paperback ed.,   op
          Univ. of Nebraska Pr., 1961)

I have tried to tell not only the story of the man but something of the life of his people through that crucial time.

The epic story of a greathearted, courageous chief is strangely filled with a foreboding of impending doom. The author wrote with power, beauty, and passion of the Oglala Sioux people whom she, from her childhood at the edge of the Indian country, had greatly admired. Based on thorough research, including interviews with He Dog, Crazy Horse's lifelong brother-friend, this biography is as accurate and comprehensive as orally transmitted sources could make it. In this vigorous and passionate work the author hoped to convey Indian concepts for which no English equivalents exist.

212 Sandoz, Mari. *Old Jules.* Little, 1935. 424p.   (S)
    (Reprint ed., Hastings, 1975) (Paperback ed., Univ.
    of Nebraska Pr., 1962)

> This country will develop—in time. . . . But not until the ground is soaked in misery and in blood.

Mari Sandoz's biography of her father, Jules Sandoz, was written at his request to record his contributions to the building and settlement of Nebraska. Not only is it the story of her father's life, it is also a sensitive history of the entire state. Combining generosity, meanness, callousness, respect for his fellow settlers, and contempt for cowards or weaklings, Old Jules is an extremely complex personality. These facets of his character are presented at various times with equal vigor. The resulting story is one of a man whose foresight could be respected, even though his actions could not always be admired.

213 Sanford, Mollie Dorsey. *Mollie.* Univ. of Nebraska   (S)
    Pr., 1959. 201p. (Paperback ed., 1976)

> Father had named the place "Hazel Dell" and we christened it by singing that sweet song.

The journal of a young woman whose father moved his family to Nebraska Territory in 1857 reflects the hopes and subsequent despair of those who left homes and friends to seek their fortune in a rugged country. Homesteading on the Little Nemaha meant a crowded cabin and the threat of rattlesnakes, but Mollie found much to make her content. When marriage took her on a difficult wagon trek across the plains to Colorado, she longed to return to Hazel Dell, the family home. The book contains an excellent account of the Colorado Gold Rush and of army life in the pioneer West.

214 Sergeant, Elizabeth Shepley. *Willa Cather: A*   (S)
    Memoir. Lippincott, 1953. 288p. (Paperback ed.,   op
    Univ. of Nebraska Pr., 1963)

Willa used to tell me about the Christmas boxes to these long loved and remembered Nebraska families.

The close friendship between Willa Cather and Elizabeth Sergeant made possible an intimate picture, full of anecdotes and written in an appealing, informal style. After taking a swift look backward to note Willa's girlhood, Sergeant concentrates on the years 1910 to 1931, then briefly recounts incidents of Willa's life until she died in 1947. In addition to valuable assessments of Cather's major works, the book reveals much of the Nebraska prairie life so authentically portrayed in Cather's novels.

215 Sevareid, Eric. *Not So Wild a Dream.* Knopf, 1947.   (S)
516p.   op

So far as Velva was concerned, wheat was the sole source and meaning of our lives.

The first fifty pages of this book are devoted to North Dakota, and particularly to Velva, where Sevareid lived until he attended the University of Minnesota. First-rate reporting of World War II, the military fatuity, the bumbling, and the waste of lives follows. Sevareid used autobiography not to memorialize his life but to enrich the common experience and provide a vehicle for his thoughts and interpretation of life.

216 Seymour, Flora Warren. *Bird Girl: Sacagawea.*   (I)
Illus. by Edward C. Caswell. Bobbs-Merrill, 1945.   op
187p.

As for me, I shall go on to the setting sun with my husband and the party of Americans.

Sacagawea's lifelong desire was to travel to faraway places. As a small child, she dreamed of finding the tepee of the sun. As a woman, she led Lewis and Clark to the shores of the Pacific, "the great salty water." The author has written a somewhat didactic but interesting version of the Bird Woman's role in the exploration and discovery of the West.

217 Slaughter, Linda Warfel. *Linda W. Slaughter's*   (J, S)
Fortress to Farm; or Twenty-three Years on the   op
Frontier. Exposition, 1972. 172p.

It is impossible to describe . . . the dreadful feeling of solitude and impending danger that deepened as we steamed further and further up the river.

Linda Slaughter exchanged a life of ease and luxury in Tennessee for life as the wife of an Army surgeon in the unsettled Dakota Territory. Her colorful, eyewitness account of her own eventful experiences, sometimes dangerous, parallels the development of the area and the settlement of the city of Bismarck in 1872.

218   Slote, Bernice. *Willa Cather.* Illus. by Lucia Woods   (I, J, S)
and others.   Univ. of Nebraska Pr., 1973.   134p.

> The colors and shapes and voices of the land are there, not reported but recreated.

The real and imagined world of Willa Cather is presented in a striking combination of photos and text which reveals the vivid memories of people and places that shaped her creative genius. Her early life in Red Cloud is detailed in Part I. Included in Part II, "Willa Cather's America," are the Midlands, which provided the setting for *O Pioneers!* and *My Ántonia,* recreated in color illustrations, quotes from her novels, and explanatory text. This stimulating work includes many family photographs.

219   Snyder, Albert B., and Yost, Nellie Snyder. *Pinnacle*   (S)
Jake.   Univ. of Nebraska Pr., 1951.   255p.   op
(Paperback ed., 1962)

> When they got to the old cabin they found the cowboy in there, setting in a chair, froze to death.

The early life of Pinnacle Jake Snyder was spent on a Nebraska homestead, but his cowboy career began in 1887 at the age of fifteen when he headed for the Ogallala Land and Cattle Company with a bunch of saddle horses. He started as a night wrangler at forty dollars a month and regretted that he later turned down Bill Cody's offer to take him to England in the Wild West Show. The dangers and hard work of life on the ranch and range are vividly portrayed, yet many humorous anecdotes enliven the account.

220   Snyder, Grace. *No Time on My Hands.*   Caxton,   (J, S)
1963.   541p.   op

> If there's one thing more 'n another I simply can't abide, it's time on my hands.

Growing up on a central Nebraska homestead just before the turn of the century allowed the author little opportunity for time on her hands. Although the demands of six sisters and two brothers were many, she did find time to fulfill her three goals in life: to make the most beautiful quilts in the world, to marry a cowboy, and to look down on the top of a cloud. While the ponderous length and intricate details of family history may make some sections tedious for young readers unless read aloud, the easy, conversational tone will please the more mature. The optimistic realism of the story avoids falseness and may prompt discussion of the reality of homesteading on the prairie. Photographs of the Snyder family illustrate the story.

221 Stith, Forrest M. *Sunrises and Sunsets for Freedom.* (J, S)
Vantage, 1973. 89p.

> It is not in him [man] to direct his steps, and he must look to the Lord our God.

Nebraska's promise of cheap, rich land appealed to both well-established and displaced persons. Many former slaves living a frugal existence in Canada accepted the challenge of homesteading in Nebraska with the goal of "proving-up" the land and building permanent homes. The author's ancestors were part of this movement. He traces his family's story from the time of the frantic grab for freedom and flight to Canada to settlement in Dawson County, Nebraska, and shows the inner motivations. Although the tone is biblical and at times the family details are tedious enough to cool the interest of younger readers, many who are seeking a different point of view may appreciate this story.

222 Syme, Ronald. *The Story of Pierre de la Verendrye,* (I)
Fur Trader of the North. Illus. by Richard Cuffari. op
Morrow, 1973. 191p.

> France must make a search for some navigable inlet that leads perhaps to the Western Sea. . . . Each step will be marked by a trading post.

Pierre de la Verendrye accepted the governor's challenge to expand the knowledge of the western territory of New France. In June 1727, he left his home to begin his exploration of the interior of North America, to search for a passage to the Pacific, and to set up fur trading posts. Explorations were made by de la Verendrye or his men into North Dakota, South Dakota, Montana, and Wyoming. This interesting account of his life relates his struggle for financial help, the difficulties of exploration, and his determination to succeed.

223 Thompson, Era Bell. *American Daughter.* Univ. of (J, S)
Chicago Pr., 1946. 300p. (Reprint ed., Follett, 1967. op
296p.) (Paperback ed., Univ. of Chicago Pr., 1974)

> Now there were fifteen of us, four per cent of the state's entire Negro population.

As a small child, Era Bell Thompson moved with her family to Driscoll, North Dakota. There were few blacks among the sparse population of North Dakota in the early twentieth century. The Thompson family not only farmed in Driscoll but also lived in Bismarck and

Mandan. Era Bell attended the University of North Dakota in Grand Forks. The book concludes with the author's experiences in Chicago as a young woman. The treatment of blacks is described matter-of-factly.

224 Tweton, D. Jerome. *The Marquis de Morès: Dakota*   (S)
          Capitalist, French Nationalist. North Dakota Institute
          for Regional Studies, 1972. 249p.

>   The editor of the *Bismarck Tribune* in 1879 advertised the high plains with a steady display of testimonials and statistics.

Because of such advertising, the Marquis de Morès, discontented with the meaningless life of a French nobleman, left France to make a home for himself in America. He built facilities for cattle raising and meat packing near the Little Missouri River at Medora, which he named in honor of his wife. When his business empire crumbled, the Marquis returned to Europe to become France's most outspoken nationalist.

225 Van Nuys, Laura Bower. *The Family Band: From*   (S)
          the Missouri to the Black Hills 1881–1900. (Pioneer
          Heritage) Univ. of Nebraska Pr., 1962. 256p.

>   Father says we shall have to get a new organ. Mother says we can't cook on an organ. She thinks that the first thing to get when we get into a house of our own should be a cook stove.

The Bower family survived the 1881 Vermillion flood in which Od's organ floated away down the Missouri, a wagon trek across Dakota Territory to the Black Hills, and an assortment of natural disasters common to homesteaders. They maintained a song in their hearts and made music wherever they went. The author, youngest of nine children, tells of her father's borrowing money to buy his children musical instruments and of their playing at every celebration in Rapid City and the surrounding area. Walt Disney based a movie, *The One and Only, Genuine, Original Family Band,* on this book.

226 Veglahn, Nancy. *The Buffalo King: The Story of*   (J)
          Scotty Philip. Illus. by Donald Carrick. Scribner,   op
          1971. 180p.

>   "The buffalo have come back to us. Now we can all be happy again," the old man said.

Scotty Philip heard his wife's aged uncle, One Eye, say that the buffalo had returned, but he knew it was not true. Actually only a few buffalo remained on the prairie. Scotty, a Scottish immigrant, lived an adventurous life as farmer, gold prospector, army scout, shipper, and rancher. However, his greatest success was in preserving the magnificent plains buffalo from extinction by developing his own buffalo herd. For this endeavor he was nicknamed "Buffalo King."

227   Vestal, Stanley. *Sitting Bull, Champion of the Sioux.* (S)
Houghton, 1932. 352p. (New ed., Univ. of   op
Oklahoma Pr., 1957) (Reprint ed., 1976)

> No man in the Sioux nation was braver than Sitting Bull.

This stirring account of the death throes of a mighty nation and its leader is the story of the "greatest of the Sioux" and his struggle to keep his people free and united. The Sioux were the best cavalry in the world, but they faced an overwhelming tide of soldiers, homesteaders, and bureaucrats. The victory over Custer at the Battle of the Little Big Horn demonstrated their organization. Although Sitting Bull was one of the most visionary of statesmen, he could not prevail against the odds.

228   Voight, Virginia Frances. *Sacajawea.* Illus. by Erica (P)
Merkling. (A See and Read Beginning to Read
Biography) Putnam, 1967. 63p.

> "We will name her for the swans," he said. So the Indian princess was named Sacajawea, which means Bird Woman.

Simply, yet effectively, the author and artist have collaborated to tell the tale of the Shoshone Indian woman who knew the Shining Mountains well enough to guide Captain Lewis and Captain Clark through the deep forests and over the trails to the Pacific Ocean. Captured by the Minnetaree in her childhood, she had missed the tall trees and cold streams of her home and was happy to return. A list of key words and a pronunciation guide of Indian names are appended.

229   Welk, Lawrence, and McGeehan, Bernice. (S)
Wunnerful, Wunnerful: The Autobiography of   op
Lawrence Welk. Prentice-Hall, 1971. 294p.
(Paperback ed., Bantam, 1973)

> Music pulled at me continually. Everything about it fascinated me.

Lawrence Welk's early life was spent near Strasburg, North Dakota. The one-night stands of his band in North and South Dakota at the outset of his career highlight descriptions of life in small rural towns of the plains in the 1920s. Although much of Lawrence Welk's life has been spent far from Strasburg, he indicates that the homely and enduring values he learned there helped him to reach impressive personal achievement without losing humility. This Horatio Alger-type story presents a likeable, shrewd man.

230   Werenstein, Irving. *Marshall without a Gun, Tom* (J, S)
Smith. Messner, 1959. 192p.   op

> Mayor Henry spoke . . . "Go home men! There's been enough bloodshed." The mob broke up. Law had come to Abilene.

Tom Smith, a Kansas lawman never glamorized on television or in movies, was a giant in his time. He brought law and order to Abilene, using his fists instead of a gun. A memorial marker was placed on his grave in 1904 after Abilene had become a quiet prairie town. Students will appreciate this exciting approach to Kansas history.

231   White, William Allen.   *The Autobiography of William*   (S)
Allen White.   Macmillan, 1946.   669p.

> I haven't seen as much sense in one column in a dozen years.

Thomas Reed, Speaker of the U.S. House of Representatives, wrote the above statement, treasured by White, in response to White's editorial, "What's the Matter with Kansas." That editorial marked the beginning of public recognition of the distinguished Kansan journalist's talents in social criticism. White's autobiography preserves his keen insight into issues, presents characterizations of such leaders as Mark Hanna and Theodore Roosevelt, and includes the poignant "Mary White." The book was awarded the Pulitzer Prize in 1947.

232   Wilder, Laura Ingalls.   *On the Way Home: The*   (J, S)
Diary of a Trip from South Dakota to Mansfield,
Missouri, in 1894.   Harper, 1962.   101p.   (Paperback
ed., 1976)

> July 17, 1894. Camped by a spring that cannot be pumped, but there is feed for the horses. Grain about 8 inches high, will go about 1½ bushels to the acre. Hot wind.

Thus the daily notes of Laura Ingalls Wilder in a five-cent memorandum book chronicle the forty-six-day journey from De Smet, South Dakota, to "The Land of the Big Red Apple." The recollections of Rose Wilder Lane, who was seven at the time of her parents' migration, serve as a framework for the text. Photographs provide realism, and incidents such as the misplaced money will intrigue *Little House* fans.

233   Woodward, Mary Dodge.   *The Checkered Years.*   (J, S)
Caxton, 1937.   265p.   (Reprint ed., Cass County (N.   op
Dak.) Historical Society, 1976)

> The weather is extremely cold, and in spite of a good fire, we had to fetch our breakfast into the sitting room. I cooked it with my hood, shawl and mittens on.

This diary, edited by Mary Boynton Cowdrey, recounts both the joys and hardships of life on a bonanza farm in Dakota Territory from 1883 to 1887. This work becomes a reference source for everyday life in its descriptions of the harsh weather, the field crops, the farm animals, the potted flowers the author nursed through cold winters, the clothes worn, the food preparation for the threshers, and the family recreations, as well as her observations on the social customs of the time.

234 Wyman, Walker D. *Frontier Woman: The Life of a*   (S)
Woman Homesteader on the Dakota Frontier. Illus.   op
by Helen B. Wyman. River Falls Pr., 1972. 115p.

> I only knew that my husband wanted to seek our fortune on that
> new frontier. So I packed up and without looking behind, boarded the
> Northwestern Railroad for Pierre, April 6, 1902. For better or for
> worse, I had made my bed.

Grace Fairchild went from Wisconsin to Parker, South Dakota, to
teach school in 1898. At Parker she married a widower much older than
she, and together they homesteaded on the stage road half way between
Pierre and the Black Hills. Here are all the elements of fascinating
pioneer history: claim shanties, rattlesnakes, droughts, dances, churning
butter, making sauerkraut, and always the indomitable spirit of a
frontier woman. A special treat is provided by "sayings" liberally scattered throughout the text: "It was so cold that I saw two jackrabbits
pushing a cottontail to get him started." Original notes and letters provided the source material for the work.

235 Yost, Nellie Snyder, ed. *Boss Cowman: The*   (J, S)
Recollections of Ed Lemmon, 1857–1946. (The
Pioneer Heritage Series) Univ. of Nebraska Pr., 1969.
321p. (Paperback ed., 1974)

> Since I had been born and raised in the West, I was always on the
> alert.

Ed Lemmon's description of his life as a cowboy and rancher
reads almost like a script for a cowboy movie. The rancher's existence
on the Nebraska prairie during the transition from open range to home-
steads was an exciting if hazardous and sometimes violent one. The
detailed description of this flamboyant era flows easily in a conversational tone, often mentioning the names of the West's most famous or
notorious characters, such as Wild Bill Hickok, Doc Middleton, Bat
Masterson, and Chief Red Cloud. Well-documented footnotes fill in
historic details, and the index helps the researcher seeking facts about
Nebraska's wilder days.

236 Zochert, Donald. *Laura: The Life of Laura Ingalls*   (J, S)
Wilder. Regnery, 1976. 260p. (Paperback ed.,
Avon Books, 1977)

> "Running through all the stories," she said, "like a golden thread,
> is the same thought of the values of life."

Just as Laura put courage, self-reliance, independence, integrity,
helpfulness, cheerfulness, and humor into her life, she put them into her
books. This biography of the author of the *Little House* books is care-

fully researched, written with affection, and resembles the Wilder books in style. Chapters are devoted to the Big Woods, the prairie, Plum Creek, Burr Oak, Walnut Grove, and Silver Lake. Appendixes include a chronology of important dates in her life, an essay on the truth of the *Little House* books, a directory listing sites for the traveler to visit, and sources from which one may obtain additional Wilder information.

OTHER INFORMATIONAL BOOKS

237 Adams, Samuel Hopkins. *The Santa Fe Trail.* Illus.   (I, J)
by Lee J. Ames. (Landmark Books) Random, 1951.
181p.

> A western trek was started which increased steadily . . . until it changed the history of two nations.

Captain William Becknell realized the trade potential in Santa Fe during his first visit there with a small group who carried merchandise on pack mules. When he returned home, he made plans to take a caravan of wagons to Santa Fe, although "no wheel had ever turned beyond the Missouri River." A realistic account is given of the treacherous trip, much of it through Kansas. Familiar Kansas scenes will bring young readers close to these travelers in the early 1800s.

238 Alberts, Francis Jacobs, ed. *Sod House Memories,*   (J, S)
vols. 1–3. (Sod House Society Series) Sod House
Society, 1973. 285p.

> When we found a snake in the house one day it was the last straw.

The life of a homesteader was not made easier by the prospect of living in a sod house. Earth walls provided a haven for burrowing animals and crawling snakes, and every rainstorm proved to be a mud-soaked disaster. However, the sturdy sod house was the most practical form of shelter on the treeless plains, and with resourcefulness, a surprising degree of comfort was achieved. Consisting of members who lived during the sod house era or who are preserving the history of that time, the Sod House Society presents these personal accounts which include many details of sod house and prairie life in general. The specific facts concerning pioneer families will be irrelevant for the reader seeking general information, but the illustrations, photographs, and maps provide an informative look at pioneer life. An index is included.

239 Alston, Eugenia. *Come Visit a Prairie Dog Town.*   (P)
Illus. by St. Tamara. (A Let Me Read Book)
Harcourt, 1976. 60p. (Paperback ed., 1976)

Standing on their mounds, the prairie dogs are always watching.

Detailed drawings aid immeasurably in presenting the life cycle of the prairie dog. The importance of family life in the struggle for survival is emphasized in this informative, easy-to-read account.

240 Bailey, Bernadine. *Picture Book of Kansas.* Illus. by   (I)
Kurt Wiese. Rev. ed.   (United States Books)
Whitman, 1969. 32p.

The name Kansas comes from a Sioux Indian word meaning People of the South Wind.

Beginning in 1541 with the coming of the Spanish adventurers, this valuable, concise account records important events, skillfully selected to give a brief yet relatively complete picture of the state. Illustrations in both color and black and white include a map, state symbols, and typical Kansas scenes. Explorers, pioneer days, industries, and prominent citizens are identified through simple text and brief indexing.

241 Bailey, Bernadine. *Picture Book of Nebraska.* Illus.   (I)
by Kurt Wiese. Rev. ed.   (United States Books)
Whitman, 1966. 32p.

Nebraska lies "out where the West begins."

Including details on geography, state emblems, famous persons, and landmarks, this compact volume is an excellent overview of Nebraska. The discussions of these subjects are necessarily brief, but the work is easy to comprehend and will provide an appropriate beginning for young readers. The text is colorfully illustrated with drawings as well as photographs and maps.

242 Bailey, Bernadine. *Picture Book of North Dakota.*   (I)
Illus. by Kurt Wiese. Rev. ed.   (United States Books)
Whitman, 1971. 32p.

A state with a promising future, North Dakota will always be a place where people have the warm friendly spirit of the early pioneers.

The text includes a general view of the geographical features, basic highlights of its history, outstanding contributions of a few notable people, and information on some of the larger communities. Although the author's descriptions are neither animated nor detailed, this book will serve as an introductory survey.

243 Bailey, Bernadine. *Picture Book of South Dakota.*   (I)
Illus. by Kurt Wiese. Rev. ed.   (United States Books)
Whitman, 1966. 32p.

The word *Dakota* means "allies" or "friends"—a good name for a hardy, pioneering state where friendliness comes naturally.

Since the illustrations make up only half of its content, this work is not really a picture book. The very brief text includes information on the state's physical features, history, agriculture, and industry, as well as a thumbnail sketch of each major city. A map, illustrations of the state flower and state seal, and an index are special features.

244 Barns, Cass Grove. *The Sod House.* Univ. of   (J, S)
Nebraska Pr., 1970. 287p. (Paperback ed.)

Nebraska's first homesteaders were a hardy set.

Reflecting upon the activities of Nebraska pioneers in the early years of statehood, the author presents sod house living, the perils of grasshoppers and drought, and the blizzard of 1888. The book is not distinguished, but the biographical sketches of a pioneer teacher, prairie preachers, poets, doctors, and even the "money-loaner" make this a valuable resource.

245 Beine, George Holmes. *Land of the Coyote.* Iowa   (S)
State Univ. Pr., 1972. 193p.

Not only was [our homestead] not the farm of our dreams, but it also lacked any resemblance to any farm of our imaginations.

In March 1907, fourteen-year-old George Beine and his two brothers moved with their parents from Omaha to a homestead near Kimball, South Dakota. They had no livestock. The farm buildings were weatherbeaten, warped, and generally open to winds, dust, and snow. As their Pa was not a farmer, he did not know which machinery to buy, how to prepare the soil, what to plant, or when to plant it. Although he depended for survival on the guidance of neighbors, Pa was not compatible with them. While chiefly an account of George's experiences as a farmhand, horse tamer, sodbuster, and thresher, the pioneer life and times are also revealed.

246 Bennett, Estelline. *Old Deadwood Days.* Sears,   (S)
1928. 300p.   op

Deadwood and I grew up together through stagecoach and school days until the railroad came in and I cried my way east to boarding school.

The author was the daughter of the first federal judge appointed to the Deadwood district of the Black Hills in 1877. As a child she was a contemporary of such famous frontier characters as Deadwood Dick, Calamity Jane, Wild Bill Hickok, Preacher Smith, and of such lesser dignitaries as Slippery Sam, Colorado Charlie, and California Jack. Her vivid memory of prospectors and sky pilots, of dance halls and theaters, and of stagecoach holdups and justice provided the raw material for this informal, anecdotal record. It has been described as "one of the most engrossing stories of the West ever written." The index increases the usability of this work.

247   Bjorklund, Lorence F.   *Faces of the Frontier.* (Men   (I, J)
       and Women of the American Frontier West) Dodd,
       1967.   119p.

> The frontier had certainly waned when I was a boy, but there was enough of it remaining all over the West so that if you leaned on anything some of it would rub off on you.

The artist/author moves as close as he can to people of the frontier to "see the features usually obscured in the shadow of their wide-brimmed hats." Here is a melting pot of frontiersmen: the Indian, the stage driver, the sheepherder, the sodbuster, the cowboy, the claim jumper, the engineer, the doctor, and the sheriff. Fifty-four detailed penciled portraits with accompanying one-page text help to make the West of the nineteenth century a reality. History or art classes will find the book particularly useful.

248   Blasingame, Ike.   *Dakota Cowboy: My Life in the Old*   (S)
       Days.   Illus. by John Mariani.   Putnam, 1958.   317p.   op
       (Paperback ed., Univ. of Nebraska Pr., 1964)

> The vanguard of the Matador left Texas and began arriving at Evarts, South Dakota, in May of 1904—and I was with them.

Thus the author, a cowboy with the Matador Land and Cattle Company, begins his story of seven years on the open range in the area of the Cheyenne Indian Reservation. A zesty, human, authentic story of every phase of the cattle business is presented with plenty of frontier humor. Endpapers feature a map of the Dakota Reservation Range locating ranches by their appropriate brands—Turkey Tracks, H A T, HO, and the like.

249   Bleeker, Sonia.   *The Sioux Indians: Hunters and*   (I, J)
       Warriors of the Plains.   Illus. by Kisa Sasaki.
       Morrow, 1962.   160p.

> The Sioux Indians, the greatest warriors of the plains, today call North and South Dakota their homelands.

This sixteenth book in the author's works on Indian tribes is a factual account of almost every detail of Sioux life. Their tribal history, search for a religious vision, dependence on the buffalo, wars and raids against other tribes, and games and festivals are identified. The last chapter details the changes that took place with the coming of the white man. Current problems are briefly summarized. An index is included.

250 Branch, Edward Douglas. *The Hunting of the* (J, S)
Buffalo. Univ. of Nebraska Pr., 1962. 240p.
(Paperback ed.)

> The wholesale butchery of buffaloes upon the plains is as needless as it is cruel.

It was said that the history of the buffalo was as scattered as the buffalo bones, and the author's purpose was to organize the information. He discusses the habits and characteristics of buffalo as well as the many hunts over Kansas plains. Much coverage is given to the people involved in the drama of destruction. The efforts in Washington to save the animals end this account of an important period in Kansas history.

251 Brand, Wayne L., and Hector, James G., eds. *North* (I, J, S)
Dakota Decision Makers. Illus. by David L. Christy. op
Analytical Statistics, 1972. 239p.

> A description and directory of political and governmental people together with general information on the state.

A brief history and chronology from 1682 to 1972 and general information of the geography, agriculture, industry, and government are presented in capsule format. There are directories of North Dakotans in national government, state and county officials, political party functionaries, and famous citizens. Many photographs, maps, and charts are included. The directory information is current for 1972.

252 *Brevet's North Dakota Historical Markers and Sites.* (I, J)
Illus. by Gail J. Smith. Brevet Pr., 1975. 166p.
(Paperback ed., 1975)

> The book should prove to be of considerable assistance to those wishing to study North Dakota history on location where the events took place.

The early pioneers kept history alive by erecting historical markers throughout the state. This book combines the marker texts and their locations with the historical photographs, drawings, and maps to produce a living North Dakota history. A thorough index provides easy access to information.

253 *Brevet's South Dakota Historical Markers.* Brevet (S)
Pr., 1974. 285p. (Paperback ed., 1975)

> "You are now entering South Dakota. . . . Welcome to our state."

Since 1951 the South Dakota State Historical Society, the State Highway Department, and various interested individuals and firms have erected over 450 markers on the sites of those events which made a significant contribution to the history of the state. This book locates each marker by map and by highway, quotes the inscription on the marker, and adds appropriate photos or sketches. County, illustration, and marker indexes are included. The publisher's companion wall map, numerically locating all markers, provides further means for map reading and history activities.

254 *Broken Hoops and Plains People: A Catalogue of*   (J, S)
      Ethnic Resources in the Humanities: Nebraska and
      Surrounding Area. Nebraska Curriculum
      Development Center, 1976. 438p.

> Each culture . . . makes some sacrifice for the greatness it achieves, and the greatness cannot be achieved without . . . sacrifice.

With its promise of land and room to grow, Nebraska provided a tempting invitation to thousands of members of various ethnic groups to settle in a land which would allow them to cling to their own customs and culture. The titles of the individual chapters demonstrate these wishes: "Germans from Russia—A Place to Call Home"; "Scandinavians—The Search for Zion"; and "Czechs—The Love of Liberty." The Irish, Blacks, Indians, Chicanos, Jews, Italians, Dutch, and Japanese are also represented in chapters dealing with their cultures. Prejudice against these groups as well as their eventual adaptation to a new land while clinging to their ethnic identity is discussed openly and honestly. Statistical information and a bibliography follow each chapter. Photographs illustrate the text.

255 Burns, Paul C., and Hines, Ruth. *To Be a Pioneer.*   (I)
      Illus. by Frank Aloise. Abingdon, 1962. 111p.

> Instead of complaining about the things he did not have, [the pioneer] found ways of using the materials around him to supply his needs.

To be a pioneer meant to be resourceful. This small book outlines instructions for dipping candles, braiding rugs, making soap, drying apples, churning butter, making cottage cheese, and dancing "Skip to My Lou." The material should inspire many creative activities.

256 Caras, Roger A. *The Custer Wolf: Biography of an*   (S)
      American Renegade. Illus. by Charles Fracé. Little,   op
      1966. 175p.

> Lobo went to his haunches, faced the heavens, and called to the world his woe of magnificent proportions.

Lobo, the Custer wolf, was one of the most destructive of the predators whose forays cost western stockmen between twenty and thirty million dollars per year between 1915 and 1920. With a reputation for having killed thirty heads of cattle in a single week, this white wolf became the object of a massive hunt in a radius of thirty miles from Custer, South Dakota. He was finally trapped and shot by H. P. Williams in 1920. The wolf's life, habits, and instincts are reconstructed in this sensitively told story of his struggle for survival.

257   Carpenter, Allan. *Kansas.* Illus. by Roger   (I)
      Herrington. (Enchantment of America) Childrens
      Pr., 1965. 93p.

> Kansas is one of the finest sources of fossil remains.

Simple vocabulary is used to give young readers a brief introduction to the Kansas of yesterday and today. Information on historical background, natural and human resources, education, and industries is well presented. Among the interesting situations which are recorded is the English settlement's attempt to dam Big Creek near Victoria. They planned to have enough water for a steamboat which was brought overland by oxcart. The attempt as well as the settlement failed.

258   Carpenter, Allan. *North Dakota.* Illus. by Roger   (I)
      Herrington. (Enchantment of America) Childrens
      Pr., 1968. 95p.

> Principal tourist attraction of North Dakota is . . . Theodore Roosevelt National Memorial Park.

Carpenter begins by telling us something about the geological formation of the land. He proceeds to prehistoric times, then to the Indians, the explorations, the trappers, traders, and settlers. The wildlife, the products of the rich soil, minerals, and transportation within the state are discussed. The people and their educational institutions are described. Finally, the trademark of the series, "The Enchantment of North Dakota," forms the final chapter in which highlights of the larger cities and other points of interest are described.

259   Casey, Robert J. *The Black Hills and Their*   (S)
      Incredible Characters: A Chronicle and a Guide.   op
      Bobbs-Merrill, 1949. 383p.

> There is no mountain area anywhere that offers so great a variety of such interesting things in so small a space.

In part a history, in part a guidebook, this fascinating book presents anecdotes of the famous and the infamous whose lives and legends form the Black Hills story. Wild Bill Hickok, Calamity Jane, Deadwood Dick, Fly Specked Billy, Poker Alice, General Custer, Gutzon Borglum, and Sitting Bull are among those included. An extensive appendix, bibliography, and index increase its usefulness.

260   Clark, Champ.   *The Badlands*.   (The American   (J, S)
Wilderness) Time-Life, 1975.   184p.

It is a confusing land, a disturbing land, full of strange and scalded
shapes.

Visitors to Badlands National Monument and armchair explorers
will echo the author's pride, peace, and wonderment as he walked over
its eroded surfaces. The geological and meteorological past as well as
the plant and animal life are vividly depicted in text and colored photographs. Theodore Roosevelt's role as a rancher in this great wilderness
is portrayed. An index enhances the reference value.

261   Coe, Edith C.   *Hertzler Heritage*.   Emporia State   (S)
Pr., 1975.   172p.   (Paperback ed., 1975)

A Health Museum for Kansas has been the dream for a number of
years.

The dream was realized in 1965 when the only rural health museum in the world opened in Halstead, Kansas. Dr. Irene Koeneke
Hertzler, wife of Halstead's "horse and buggy doctor," Arthur E.
Hertzler, has seen the establishment of the Kansas Health Museum and
Hertzler Research Foundation as a memorial to her husband and a
service to the people of Kansas. Her concentrated, untiring efforts and
the assistance of colleagues, friends, and interested persons working
for a common goal are presented here in a valuable historical record.

262   Collins, Joseph T.   *Amphibians and Reptiles in Kansas*.   (I, J, S)
(Public Education Series) Univ. of Kansas Museum of
Natural History, 1974.   283p.   (Paperback ed.)

Knowledge of these creatures will better enable us to understand
and appreciate the prairies and woodlands of Kansas.

The importance of amphibians and reptiles as an integral part of
the Kansas fauna is emphasized. The 103 photographs help identify
salamanders, frog and toad species, turtles, lizards, and snakes. Description, size, habitat, food, and breeding information are provided;
rare or endangered species also are indicated. The book will be of value
to the general reader as well as to the biologist. Other selected titles
from this series will also be useful in Kansas collections.

263   Costello, David F.   *The World of the Prairie Dog*.   (I, J, S)
(Living World) Lippincott, 1970.   160p.

I'd rather have a few prairie dogs in the south forty than a rock
from the moon in my front yard.

Native Kansans who have enjoyed watching prairie dog communities will appreciate this attractive book with its excellent photo-

graphs by the author. Extensive coverage is given to species, social structure, and habits of this familiar prairie animal.

264   Crabb, Richard.   *Empire on the Platte.*   Illus. by   (S)
         Ernest L. Reedstrom.   World, 1967.   373p.   op

   The east-west lifeline of the United States was, and is, through the Platte Valley.

In this readable volume the author attempts to bring the vital significance of the Platte River and its valley into clear perspective. The Pony Express, the telegraph, and the first transcontinental railroad all had routes along its river banks. Known as "a valley of decision," the area has also been the site of numerous power struggles between the Indians and the pioneers, the cattlemen and the homesteaders. One dispute with far-reaching implications was between the Olive family, cattlemen, and Luther Mitchell and Ami Ketchum, homesteaders. After the murders of Mitchell and Ketchum, Governor Nance intervened, bringing the cattle king, Print Olive, and his confederates to justice and opening the area for settlement. Black-and-white photographs add to the interest value.

265   Cross, Frank B., and Collins, Joseph T.   *Fishes in*   (J, S)
         Kansas.   (Public Education Series) Univ. of Kansas
         Museum of Natural History, 1975.   189p.

   Thirty million dollars a year are spent by approximately one third of the Kansas population on fishing activities.

Although identifying Kansas fish and locating them in Kansas waters is the major purpose of the work, environmental factors affecting fish population and distribution as well as man's effect on fishes are discussed. Concise information on each species includes description, habitat, reproduction, and food. An excellent map shows locations of reservoirs completed, those under construction, and others planned. A map of the state shows counties and streams where fish are found. Extensive bibliographies are provided.

266   Davis, Kenneth S.   *Kansas: A Bicentennial History.*   (S)
         (The States and the Nation) Norton, 1976.   226p.

   This state has an impact and hold upon the minds and hearts of its people that is quite remarkable.

Written as part of a bicentennial series, this work received financial support from the National Endowment for the Humanities. Of special interest and value are the sections on twentieth-century Kansas and the photographer's essay by A. Y. Owen on the present day. The bibliography will be helpful for those seeking further historical information.

267 Dick, Everett. *Sod-House Frontier, 1854–1890.*   (J, S)
Johnsen Publishing, 1954. 550p.

> Plains travel and frontier life are peculiarly severe upon women and oxen.

This highly readable and accurate description of the growth and development of the Nebraska–Kansas–Dakota area includes many first-hand accounts spiced with human-interest anecdotes. In addition to the political and economic discussion, the social aspects of the developing land are described. The relationship of the Indians to the whites is treated objectively. Photographs enhance the text; maps and the detailed index will aid young researchers who may prefer to use only portions of this lengthy book.

268 Dietrich, Irvine T., and Hove, John, eds.   (J, S)
Conservation of Natural Resources in North Dakota.
North Dakota Institute for Regional Studies, 1962.
327p.

> Conservation . . . is a science of the outdoors, including the relationship between the people and the world in which they live.

Because of the need to teach conservation in North Dakota, this book was compiled by a committee and edited for use in the schools as a text and reference book. It is an inventory of the natural resources of the state as well as a resource for basic information about their origin, utilization, and the laws that govern them.

269 Drache, Hiram M. *The Challenge of the Prairie: Life*   (S)
and Times of Red River Pioneers. North Dakota
Institute for Regional Studies, 1970. 360p.

> The pioneers . . . all had one thing in common . . . a vision for a greater life.

The life and times of the smaller landholders among the Red River pioneers were obtained from research, actual interviews, autobiographical sketches, and memoirs of the early settlers themselves. Their backgrounds were varied, but they all faced isolation and relied on their own resourcefulness and ingenuity for survival against the great challenge of prairie life. Over one hundred illustrations and photographs support the written content of this book.

270 Drache, Hiram M. *The Day of the Bonanza.* North   (S)
Dakota Institute for Regional Studies, 1964. 239p.

> Our state is to be depopulated by the "Dakota Fever" and hundreds of people are leaving constantly for the world's great wheat fields.

Statements such as the quotation appearing in newspapers published east of the Dakotas identify the appeal of bonanza farming in the Red River Valley of the North during the late 1800s. The bonanzas had immense acreages, the capital for large-scale operations, the latest agricultural machines, and a large transient labor force. A valuable collection of manuscripts enabled the author to write a detailed story of the actual operations of a bonanza farm.

271 Duffus, Robert Luther.   *The Santa Fe Trail.*   (S)
     Longmans, 1930.   283p.   (Reprint ed., McKay, 1975).
     (Paperback ed., Univ. of New Mexico Pr., 1972)

> Of all who ride under the pointing finger of fate the men who break new trails have the mightiest monuments.

The drama and romance of the Santa Fe Trail are skillfully woven into this accurate historical account which identifies the contributions of the many groups who suffered severe hardships and dangers while reaping the rewards of travel on it. Two chapters, "The Trail Makers" and "Trails of Steel," are of special interest. Inclusion of an extensive bibliography, an index, and a number of photographs and maps enhance this well-organized, useful reference tool.

272 Engel, Lorenz.   *Among the Plains Indians.*   Illus. by   (I, J, S)
     George Catlin and Karl Bodmer.   (Nature and Man)
     Lerner, 1970.   106p.

> Once, before the European settlers came, there were probably several million Indians, separated into many different tribes.

Karl Bodmer, a Swiss artist, and George Catlin, an American painter, were involved in separate expeditions into American Indian territory in the early 1800s. Both recorded their impressions on canvas, and their paintings have furnished valuable and authentic information on the native Americans of the early nineteenth century. A fictional text, based on the actual expeditions, has been combined with the two artists' paintings in this outstanding record, valuable for social studies, art, and recreational reading.

273 Erdoes, Richard.   *The Sun Dance People: The Plains*   (J, S)
     Indians, Their Past and Present.   Knopf, 1972.   218p.
     (Paperback ed., Random, 1972)

> The Plains Indians had a saying that a man's most precious possession is not his horse, his weapons, or his fine tepee, but his children.

The author's concerned attitude is revealed in this sympathetic treatment of growing up Indian. The past and present cultures of the Sun Dance people are contrasted. The society of the Plains Indians' prereservation days is well described. The obligations of the white society to the Indians today is discussed with an understanding which will beget respect and sympathy for the Indian point of view. Erdoes does not accept the traditional view of Chivington and Custer, and an examination of the approach expressed here is long overdue.

274 Faulkner, Virginia, comp. *Roundup: A Nebraska*   (J, S)
        Reader. Illus. by Elmer Jacobs. Univ. of Nebraska   op
        Pr., 1957. 493p. (Paperback ed., 1975)

> For more than a century Nebraska has been an arena of adventure and achievement.

This collection of writings presents an overview of history through consideration of such persons as General John Pershing, William Jennings Bryan, Willa Cather, George Norris, and Mari Sandoz. Their own works are included as are impressions by those who knew them. Views of the state itself are varied and range from John Gunther's "Inside Nebraska" to the opinions of Jules Verne, Oscar Wilde, Robert Louis Stevenson, and Emily Post. Such a diversified group of contributors produces a richly varied panorama of subjects.

275 Fisher, Aileen. *Arbor Day.* Illus. by Nonny   (P, I)
        Hogrogian. (Crowell Holiday Book) Crowell, 1965.
        unp.

> Treetops make green roofs for the hillsides of America. . . . America needs trees.

In an attempt to make Nebraska a more beautiful and productive land, J. Sterling Morton devised a plan which would benefit both state and nation—Arbor Day. Told in a style which young readers will handle easily, the reasons for Arbor Day and customs relating to it are explained. Ecology-minded youngsters will discover that conservation efforts are not a recent innovation.

276 Fitzpatrick, Lilian L. *Nebraska Place-Names.* Univ.   (I, J, S)
        of Nebraska Pr., 1960. 227p. (Paperback ed., 1960)   op

> Nebraska, the name of the state, is derived from an Omaha Indian name meaning "flat water."

Organized by counties, the main body of the text indicates briefly the origin of the town names within those political areas. The work also includes selections from J. T. Link's *The Origin of the Place-Names of Nebraska* (Nebraska Geological Survey, 1933) which refer in some detail to the derivation of appellations for trails, military posts, state parks, rivers, minor streams, and relief features. An index of changed names adds to the ready reference value.

277   Gilfillan, Archer B.   *Sheep: Life on the South Dakota*   (S)
      Range.   Illus. by Kurt Wiese.   Little, 1929.   272p.   op
      (Reprint ed., Univ. of Minnesota Pr., 1957. op)

>   The opportunity to live his own life in his own way—that is the
>   herder's privilege and his very great reward.

The author, a Phi Beta Kappa graduate of the University of Pennsylvania, wrote most of this book in a sheepwagon on a ranch east of
Buffalo in Harding County, South Dakota. J. Frank Dobie, in the foreword to the reprint edition noted, "With humor and grace, this sheepherder, who collected books on Samuel Pepys, tells more about sheep
dogs, sheep nature, and the sheepherder's life than any other writer I
know." The herder's associations with his boss, neighbors, and cowboys
are also included; but the book's real strength is in the personality of
its author. "Some hold that no man can herd for six months straight
without going crazy, while others maintain that a man must have been
mentally unbalanced for at least six months before he is in fit condition
to entertain the thought of herding."

278   Gladstone, Thomas H.   *The Englishman in Kansas.*   (S)
      Miller, 1857.   328p.   (Reprint ed., Univ. of Nebraska   op
      Pr., 1971)   (Paperback ed., Univ. of Nebraska Pr.,
      1971)

>   The attack and the burning of Lawrence wrought a great change
>   in popular feeling.

A correspondent of the *London Times* wrote this firsthand account
of Kansas history in 1856, but it is still considered one of the best, most
impartial records available. Gladstone became interested in the Kansas
situation when he realized that the press, the president, and lawmakers
in Washington were in sharp disagreement. He came to Kansas seeking
the truth and recorded his impressions in a highly readable book. Coverage of Indians in Kansas and accounts of frontier life are included.

279   Goble, Paul and Dorothy.   *Red Hawk's Account of*   (I)
      Custer's Last Battle.   Pantheon, 1970.   59p.

>   We won a great victory. But when you look around you today you
>   can see that that meant little. The White Men, who were then few, have
>   spread over the earth like fallen leaves driven before the wind.

Although Red Hawk is an imaginary fifteen-year-old Sioux, this
simply told, personal story is based on published accounts of the tragic
battle at Little Big Horn. The authors note that it is an incomplete picture because "an Indian only tells of what he has seen or done." The
format and illustrations add to this unusual story for children. Stylized

Indian ponies race across pages made particularly appealing with wide margins and one column of large print. Colors are bright and the designs are in the style of the drawings the warriors would make on the sides of their tipis to relate their successes. This same format is used in the Gobles' similar story of the Fetterman massacre, *Brave Eagle's Account of the Fetterman Fight* (Pantheon, 1972).

280   Goodrum, Charles.   *I'll Trade You an Elk.*   Funk   (J, S)
            & Wagnalls, 1967.   220p.

> Before he knew it he'd become the unpaid broker for the Midwest animal trading business.

The building up of the Wichita Zoo in the 1930s was an adventure for Bernie Goodrum, his staff, embarrassed wife, and reluctant son. Bernie, director of recreation and zoo manager for the city, acquired a lost pelican and lots of publicity. As a result, Wichitans came to the zoo in droves and donated vast numbers of pets. The zoo population soared, but funds remained pinched. As Bernie began trading, necessity demanded that the Goodrum family become expert in the care and feeding of animals.

281   Graber, Kay, comp.   *Nebraska Pioneer Cookbook.*   (I, J, S)
            Illus. by Peggy W. Link.   Univ. of Nebraska Pr.,
            1974.   164p.   (Paperback ed., 1974)

> In its cuisine as in its weather, Nebraska is a land of variety and extremes.

It would be impossible to read these recipes without gaining a new perspective of Nebraska pioneer life. A surprising number of ingredients permit elegant fare as well as mundane basics. Interspersed among the recipes are origins of many dishes and accounts of early settlers who used them. What reader of Bess Streeter Aldrich's *A Lantern in Her Hand* would not be at least slightly intrigued by her recipes in this book? Many other persons also are represented as this human and basic aspect of their lives is revealed. The illustrations and photographs add interest to the recipes, many of which would be possible to make in the classroom. A table for translating recipes into modern language (i.e., two gills equals one cup) is included. An index of recipes is appended.

282   Greenwood, Annie S.   *North Dakota, Frontier of*   (J, S)
            Opportunity.   Denison, 1957.   97p.   op

> North Dakota proudly lays claim to a share in the world's first International Peace Garden.

An article on the Peace Gardens is one of a number of descriptions of special areas in North Dakota. Included also are useful histories of the various institutions of higher education in the state and vignettes of famous North Dakotans. The information is useful, but the style more laudatory than matter of fact.

283 Grinnell, George Bird. *When Buffalo Ran.* Yale   (J, S)
     Univ. Pr., 1920. 114p. (Reprint ed., Univ. of   op
     Oklahoma Pr., 1966)   (Paperback ed., Univ. of
     Oklahoma Pr., 1977)

> Always as winter drew near, the camps came closer together, and the people began to make ready to start off on the hunt for buffalo.

Before the white men came, there was a natural beauty in the land and in the lives of the Plains Indians. They developed a unique wisdom about their own simple existence. As it was incorporated into their daily lives, this tribal wisdom became tribal tradition. The Indian boy Wikis, whose true story Grinnell tells, had no father to teach him; but his uncle helped to instruct him in the ways of hunting and war.

284 Hayden, Ruth Kelley. *The Time That Was.*   (J, S)
     (Western Plains Heritage Publications no. 2)   Colby   op
     (Kansas) Community College, 1973. 215p.

> A gentle, refreshing rain was then, and is now, the most delightful of sounds on the western plains.

Although specific incidents occur in Rawlins County, Kansas, the situations, life-styles, and living conditions described are typical of the midwestern frontier. Thorough research is evident in this work, and many illustrations and photographs add to its appeal. The chapter entitled "The Schoolhouse Was Little, Seldom Red" provides an excellent picture of early education. Children's activities at work and play and the woman's place on the frontier receive special coverage. Numerous personal letters and newspaper reports add authenticity.

285 Heilman, Grant, ed. *Farm Town: A Memoir of the*   (I, J, S)
     1930's. Illus. by J. W. McManigal and Grant
     Heilman. Stephen Greene Pr., 1974. 96p.
     (Paperback ed., 1974)

> You don't need a spring tonic. Spring is a tonic.

Grant Heilman, an independent photographer, purchased a collection of eight thousand Wes McManigal negatives, and recognizing their value as a record of rural farm life during the era of subsistence farming, he has used them to produce a delightful and valuable record. Tag McManigal served as Heilman's guide as they traveled rural areas and interviewed people her husband had photographed. Those who have experienced similar situations will most appreciate such comments as "I hated that [cream] separator with a purple passion."

286   Horn, Huston. *The Pioneers.* (Time-Life Books)   (J, S)
Time, 1974. 240p.

The exodus began in 1841, a stream of men, women and children pouring out of Independence, Missouri.

Illustrations of dugouts which sheltered Nebraska families, portraits of individuals posed in their best, and a series of pictures taken by photographer Solomon Butcher are among the attractive illustrations which contribute to the value of this work. One of the book's major sections, "Sodbusters in the Heartland," deals with Nebraska and the styles of life which existed during pioneer days. A Black family proud to be landowners, a harvesting crew of the 1870s, and the Howard Ruede family who kept a diary for eighteen months provide insight into the saga of the Plains region. This attractive, readable book includes a valuable bibliography.

287   Howes, Charles. *This Place Called Kansas.* Univ.   (J, S)
of Oklahoma Pr., 1952. 236p.   op

For, although Kansas is the product of fused influences and ideas . . . the synthesis here has produced something new, something different.

The story of Kansas is viewed by a man who for nearly half a century was statehouse reporter in Topeka for the *Kansas City Star.* The book is not a history, but rather a collection of entertaining and revealing anecdotes representative of the cultural and social pattern of the state. Although Kansas was known far and near for its wheat and sunflowers, of greater importance was the atmosphere in Kansas that produced a politically alert population.

288   Humble, Emma. *The Jayhawker Book.* Illus. by   (P)
Allen Downs. Lyons & Carnahan, 1935. 90p.   op
(Available through Kansas State Reading Circle)

Kansas is a good place in which to live.

This old favorite lacks literary quality but is one of the few factual books about Kansas for the beginning reader. In the first part, the state symbols—the Jayhawker, sunflower, meadowlark, cottonwood tree, and the state's seal—are simply drawn and described. Salt mines, coal mines, oil fields, farming, and education are explored. In the second part a pioneer family coming to Kansas makes a home.

289   Hunter, William C. *Beacon across the Prairie: North*   (S)
Dakota's Land-Grant College. North Dakota
Institute for Regional Studies, 1961. 309p.

Only a man with diversified talents and boundless erudition could perform his appointed tasks.

Thus wrote Dean Waldron in 1924, remembering the founding and growth of North Dakota Agricultural College. The early days were exciting and demanding of the hard-pressed faculty. The events of national and state history from 1890 to 1960 brought their problems to the struggling college; internal strife erupted several times. The college's name change took place in 1960, but most of the material in this useful reference source precedes that date.

290   Hyde, George E.   *Red Cloud's Folk: A History of the*   (S)
          Oglala Sioux Indians.   Univ. of Oklahoma Pr., 1937.   op
          331p.   (Reprint ed., 1976)

They were no longer a free people leading their own life, but a captive group who were henceforth to be coaxed or driven along the stony path toward civilization.

In this scholarly yet very readable account is presented the history of the Oglala Sioux. Their early migrations, the establishment of the Red Cloud Agency, the events leading to the 1876 tragedy, and the final removal to the Pine Ridge Agency are faithfully recorded. Official reports as well as materials obtained from the Indians themselves were used effectively in this well-researched work.

291   Ise, John.   *Sod and Stubble.*   Illus. by Howard   (J, S)
          Simon.   Wilson-Erickson, 1936.   326p.   (Paperback   op
          ed., Univ. of Nebraska Pr., 1967)

In the downward slanting lines of her mouth . . . was written the . . . determination that would not admit defeat.

Henry and Rosie Ise homesteaded on the windswept plains of western Kansas in 1873. Their story, written by their son, is one of daily heroism against such perils as grasshoppers, illnesses, prairie fires, and dust storms. Eleven of their twelve children were reared there. In this book the reader is presented a graphic picture of pioneer life without frills, embellishments, or flights of fancy.

292   Isely, Bliss.   *Early Days in Kansas.*   Eagle Printing,   (P, I)
          1927.   160p.   (Available through Kansas State   op
          Reading Circle)

Unless history is remembered it is not worth reading; and it is not remembered unless it is interesting.

Centering each story in the collection on an outstanding character, the author presents the most dramatic events in Kansas history. The inclusion of material not recorded in any other place, conversations resulting from personal interviews, and many photographs make this book from "the stone age to the barbed wire fence" especially valuable.

293 Israel, Marion. *Dakotas.* Illus. by Paul Souza. (P, I)
(Look, Read, Learn) Melmont, 1959. 31p. op

> Hunting buffaloes was dangerous work.

The buffalo hunt is the vehicle for portraying the life-style of the
Dakota Indians before the coming of the white man. Illustrations on
every page enhance the simple text. Accurate descriptions of clothing,
food preparation, and the building of the tipis contribute to the reference value.

294 Jennewein, J. Leonard, and Boorman, Jane, eds. (S)
Dakota Panorama. Dakota Territory Centennial op
Commission, 1961. 468p. (Reprint ed., Brevet Pr.,
1973) (Paperback ed., 1973)

> You are not legislating alone for today . . . but for the tens of thous-
> ands who will soon be attracted within our limits.

Dakota Territory became a reality on March 2, 1861, when President Buchanan signed the Organic Act. This pictorial history was published for the centennial observance of the event. Twenty authors (historians, professors, freelance writers) collaborated to cover such areas
as immigration, homesteading, religion, justice, newspapers, politics,
ranching, and the state's role in the Civil War. Each chapter begins with
a quotation from the initial address of Governor William Jayne to the
First Territorial Legislature. Pictures and biographies of territorial governors and delegates, an extensive "South Dakota Reading List," a
comprehensive bibliography, and a complete index are included.

295 Jones, Evan, and Editors of Time-Life Books. *The* (S)
Plains States: Iowa, Kansas, Minnesota, Missouri, op
Nebraska, North Dakota, South Dakota. (Time-Life
Library of America) Time-Life, 1968. 192p.

> The surrounding land is vast and open, as if scaled for long-striding
> giants rather than for humankind.

The well-written prose of the book's seven sections describe the
land, the Indians, immigration and settlement, the Missouri River, agriculture, small towns, and the arts. Accompanying photographs become
picture essays of such subjects as plains weather, the Rosebud Reservation Sioux, wheat farming, and the Missouri River steamboat *Sergeant
Floyd.* Special features include maps with suggested tours; lists of museums, galleries, and festivals; a sampling of pictures of native wildlife;
a statistical summary; a pronunciation glossary; a bibliography; and
an index.

296 Karolevitz, Robert F. *Challenge: The South Dakota*   (J, S)
     Story. Brevet Pr., 1975. 323p.

> A realistic textbook for studying the heritage of a bountiful land—
> where the bounty is seldom attained without a struggle.

It is the belief of the author that South Dakota's uniqueness is
based upon the independent spirit of its citizens in the face of arduous
challenges. The author approaches the state's history in a topical arrangement. Among chapter titles are "The Challenge of Wounded
Knee," "The Challenge of Gold," "The Challenge of the River," "The
Challenge of the Dirty Thirties," and "The Challenge of the Future."
From the Mound Builders to EROS, from Manuel Lisa to Tom Brokaw,
from Yankton to Mount Rushmore, this is a "people story." Well-
captioned illustrations, an extensive bibliography, and an index are
included.

297 Kaufman, Edna Ramseyer. *Melting Pot of*   (S)
     Mennonite Cookery 1874–1974. Mennonite Pr., 1974.
     372p.

> The young are so wise, they can hear the grass grow.

Typical recipes are organized according to ten cultural groups of
Mennonites who came to Kansas and the surrounding territory a century ago. Included are old favorites for preparing dumplings, cottage
cheese, breads, cookies, and borscht. Histories tracing the origins of
each group of recipes, folk stories, charming sketches, and folk verses in
German and dialect make this a book to savor. An appendix contains
such items as soapmaking, home remedies, recipes for Grandpa's salve,
and a metric conversion chart. It is an excellent source for a study of
ethnic groups in Kansas.

298 Kazeck, Melvin E. *North Dakota: A Human and*   (S)
     Economic Geography. North Dakota Institute for
     Regional Studies, 1956. 264p.

> Geography has been . . . defined . . . as "the strategy of man, space
> and resources."

The author feels that especially in North Dakota the solutions to
problems are dependent upon a knowledge of the geography of the
state. Solutions to problems such as lack of industry, a decreasing population, need for water conservation, and necessity for state planning
depend first upon a knowledge of existing conditions. This well-organized, well-indexed book provides the geographic, historic, and economic
background needed to analyze future potential.

299 Kohl, Edith Eudora. *Land of the Burnt Thigh*. Illus.   (S)
by Stephen J. Voorhies. Funk & Wagnalls, 1938.   op
296p.

> Don't 'pear to me like you gals are big enough to homestead.

The author and her sister left St. Louis in 1907 to take up their
homestead claim thirty miles from Pierre, South Dakota. After one
panic-stricken look at their 10 by 12 foot tar-paper shack, they determined to return to Missouri immediately; but they did not anticipate
prairie problems. In the end they were victorious over poor health,
prairie fires, the land companies, and the unpredictability of nature.
They assumed the proprietorship of a newspaper, a post office, a
grocery store, and an Indian trading post, all with great good humor
and courage. Edith describes her experiences as a rewarding adventure
in leadership. The derivation of the book's title is the Brule Indian
Reservation, the site of an 1815 prairie fire.

300 Kurelek, William. *A Prairie Boy's Winter*.   (I)
Houghton, 1973. 48p.

> The sun had two little snippets of rainbow some distance from it,
> just above the horizon. His father referred to this in Ukrainian: "The
> sun has ears," he said. But the other children in school with William
> knew they were called sundogs.

The artist/author grew up in the 1930s on a dairy farm in Mani-
toba not far from the United States border, an area which has much in
common with the Great Plains states. Here in twenty full-page paintings, each with an accompanying page of prose, he describes the winters of his childhood, from the fall migration of the crows to their return
in spring. Activities included are playing fox and geese, looking for
rabbit tracks, skating on the bog, hauling hay to the livestock, providing
firewood, and building houses in snowdrifts. Also useful is his *Prairie
Boy's Summer* (Houghton, 1975).

301 La Flesche, Francis. *The Middle Five*. Univ. of   (I, J)
Wisconsin Pr., 1963. 152p. (Paperback ed.)

> The boy who could not fight found it difficult to maintain the re-
> spect of his mates.

Recollections of life at the mission boarding school for the Omaha
Indians which the author attended in the 1860s are the basis for this
series of sketches the author wrote to give insight into the educational
system from the Indian point of view. The Middle Five was a group
of boys who found companionship through the hardships of giving up
their language and conforming to a rigid discipline enforced by a

hickory rod, typical in schools of that day. The students were treated as members of a Christian family, and practical training in the white man's way was part of the program. The tale ends with the illness and death of Brush, one of the five friends. Except for the addition of a few maps and the correction of typographical errors, the text follows faithfully an edition published in 1900 and subtitled *Indian Boys at School.*

302   Lauber, Patricia.   *Dust Bowl: The Story of Man on*   (I, J)
      the Great Plains.   Coward, 1958.   96p.   op
      (Reprint ed., Hale, 1958)

>   People shut their houses tight and wedged wet cloths around the windows and doors. The dust came through, blackening and clinging to everything it touched.

This factual account of the Great Plains, and particularly of the Dust Bowl, details how unwitting misuse of natural resources caused the black blizzards of the 1930s. Scientists and farmers today are seeking ways to assure that such a tragedy will not happen again. Photographs contributed by the Soil Conservation Service and maps by Wes McKeown enrich the text. A brief index is included.

303   Lewis, Faye Cashatt.   *Nothing to Make a Shadow.*   (S)
      Illus. by Lois Shelton.   Iowa State Univ. Pr., 1972.   155p.

>   "There's nothing to make a shadow," Mother said. "If we could just see some shade somewhere, it wouldn't seem quite so hot."

Mrs. Lewis reflects on her thirteenth year, 1909, when she went from Iowa with her family to their homestead in Tripp County, South Dakota. Warm and human memories of her Dakota heritage are revealed in the experiences with railroads, claim shacks, crops and prairie fires, neighbors, chores, churches, and schools. The nostalgia of a philosopher surfaces as she lovingly recalls the Dakota she once knew.

304   Lindquist, Emory.   *Bethany in Kansas: The History*   (S)
      of a College.   Bethany College, 1975.   308p.

>   The verdant prairies into blue hills rise
>   To match the sapphire glory of the skies.

The unique and distinctive contributions to Kansas made by the Lindsborg Swedes are well documented in this record of a small Kansas college. The coverage of the Messiah presentation, including its origin and development, and the information on Birger Sandzen will serve as valuable resource material. Numerous photos, maps, and songs contribute to knowledge about frontier life.

305   Long, R. W.   *Wichita Century.*   The Wichita   (J, S)
Museum Association, 1969.   277p.

> Wichita has been fortunate to have citizens from all ethnic groups
> . . . all walks of life and cultural backgrounds.

Leaders, promoters, inventors, business and professional men and
women have been willing to tie their personal fortunes and futures to
Wichita's prospects. When Wichita was born in 1870, photography was
in its infancy; but it was effective enough to make possible a photographic story of a prairie metropolis. The colorful and exciting history
of Wichita's first one hundred years is captured here in words and
pictures.

306   Lyle, Wes, and Fisher, James.   *Kansas Impressions.*   (I, J, S)
Univ. Press of Kansas, 1972.   unp.

> This is a book of discovery—an exploration of Kansas in photographs
> and words.

An outstanding interpretation of the rich resources and scenic
beauty of Kansas is presented through black-and-white photographs
by Wes Lyle and accompanying quotations collected by James Fisher.
The common image of the state as an endless, wheat-covered plain is
dispelled as the authors focus on the people and the scenery to capture
the "feel" of the state. Urban, rural, and industrial photographs are
represented. The skillfully selected quotations allow the people to
speak for their state.

307   McCracken, Harold.   *The American Cowboy.*   (S)
Doubleday, 1973.   196p.   (Paperback ed., A & W
Pubs., 1976)

> Of all the men on horseback, the American cowboy has gained the
> most widespread popular image, and that image will probably out-
> shine the others in the future.

The history of the American cowboy is chronicled from the time
of the first horses in America to the present and counteracts the fiction
of Hollywood. Here are the conquistadors of Cortes, the Mexican
vaqueros, the cattle barons, and the homesteaders and rustlers who
harrassed the cowboys of the northern plains. But more importantly,
here are reproductions of artworks by Charles M. Russell, Frederick
Remington, Edward Borein, Charles J. Belden, W. H. D. Koerner,
Frank Tenney Johnson, George Catlin, and many others which tell the
story more graphically than text can do. An index is included.

308   McKee, James L., and Duerschner, Arthur.   (I, J, S)
Lincoln: A Photographic History.   Salt Valley Pr.,
1976.   199p.

> The bicentennial era . . . offers impetus to this history of Lincoln

and Lancaster County though they are youngsters in comparison to our nation.

Youngsters or not, Lincoln, Nebraska, and Lancaster County are filled with history. From Luke Lavender's log cabin to the large, modern public library on the same site, details of people and places in Lincoln abound. This collection of photographs accompanied by a brief explanation presents the history of forgotten landmarks. Many interesting items of information are included to personalize this realistic account.

309 McKeown, Martha Ferguson. *Them Was the Days.*   (J, S)
Univ. of Nebraska Pr., 1961. 282p. (Paperback ed.)

"We had to . . . toughy it out because there wasn't nothing wrong with our sod house—or with the land we'd built her on.

The years immediately following the Civil War were difficult ones for everyone, but especially for the Hawthorne family. Their move from Pennsylvania to Virginia proved unsuccessful, and three years later they migrated to Nebraska to file claim on a homestead. Their new life had numerous frustrations which eventually were overcome. Told with frankness, the story evidences objectivity. The viewpoints presented reflect the times, and the author carefully constructs her uncle's story from his perspective and in his style.

310 McLaughlin, James. *My Friend the Indian.*   (S)
Houghton, 1910. 416p. (Reprint ed., Superior   op
Publishing, 1970)

I hold to nothing more firmly, am proud of nothing so much as of the fact that my red friends of the West have given me the title of friend.

James McLaughlin, for whom the town of McLaughlin was named, was appointed Indian Agent on Standing Rock Reservation in 1881 and was present on December 15, 1890, when Sitting Bull was killed. This book was Major McLaughlin's attempt to correct some of the misconceptions regarding the Indian then prevalent among the whites. He felt capable of this task because of the thirty-eight years he had spent "very close to the scent of tepee smoke." Although chiefly autobiographical, this account also includes events related to him by his Indian contemporaries. It is generously seasoned with references to such notables as Sitting Bull, John Grass, Spotted Tail, Chief Gall, and Chief Joseph. An index is included.

311 Marriott, Alice. *Indians on Horseback.* Illus. by   (I, J)
Margaret Lefranc. Crowell, 1948. 136p. (Rev. ed.,   op
1968)

With this discovery, that they could move around easily on horse-back, the Indians began a new way of life.

Alice Marriott, the first woman to receive a degree in anthropology from the University of Oklahoma, has lived among the Kiowa and Cheyenne Indians and is a recognized authority on Indian ethnology. Brief introductory chapters on the history of the Plains Indians and their early experiences with the whites are followed by fascinating chapters on how the Indians governed themselves, danced the Sun Dance, healed their ill, cooked their food, and made items necessary for daily living. A wealth of ideas for Indian projects can be found in the text and drawings. An index and bibliography are included.

312   Mattes, Merrill J.   *The Great Platte River Road.*   (S)
      Nebraska State Historical Society, 1969.   583p.

> The Platte River valley was largely barren of timber and was scarred by buffalo tracks, but it had three cardinal virtues . . . it was dry, it was level, and it went in exactly the right direction.

Firsthand accounts of seven hundred covered-wagon emigrants form the basis for this in-depth study of that portion of the overland trail system which followed the Platte River via Fort Kearney to Fort Laramie. Spanning the time between 1804 and the last significant wagon travel in 1866, the places and events are chronicled through the lives of the people involved. Vivid descriptions of forts, accounts of disease, and the tragedies of conflict with the Indians are recorded. Stories of unhappy fur traders and records of the thrill of discovery of a new land are part of this collective experience. An impressive bibliography of the primary and secondary sources used is appended. Authentic black-and-white photos, many historical in nature, and detailed maps orient the reader to the areas under consideration.

313   Miller, Nyle H.   *Kansas—The 34th Star.* Kansas State   (I, J, S)
      Historical Society, 1976.   153p.

> Everyone who resides in a city or town is still only a few minutes from the open space of the country.

Special funding for the American Bicentennial made possible this outstanding photographic history from the Kansas State Historical Society. A blend of effective color and black-and-white photographs, maps, and sketches depicts Kansas from its first people, the Indians, to today's inhabitants. "Doctor, Lawyer, Merchant" and "They Made Their Mark" interpret Kansas by focusing on individual personalities. The fact that each section tells its story through pictures accompanied by a minimal amount of text makes the work appropriate at several grade levels.

314   Miller, Nyle H., and Snell, Joseph W.   *Great*   (J, S)
Gunfighters of the Kansas Cowtowns, 1867–1886.
Univ. of Nebraska Pr., 1967.   476p. (Paperback ed.,
1967)

Without their antics the West might not so easily have achieved
its wild image.

Biographical accounts of twenty-one gunfighters in seven major
Kansas cowtowns were compiled from newspapers, public records,
letters, and diaries. Because old timers had a tendency to exaggerate
their own roles in events described, reminiscences were not used. Besides the material on the twenty-one individuals, the book gives an
excellent picture of life in the seven towns. Much of the material in
this excellent account of early Kansas town life first appeared in *The
Kansas State Historical Society Quarterly.* It was later expanded and
collected into *Why the West Was Wild* (Univ. of Nebraska Pr., 1967),
from which this book was excerpted.

315   Miller, Nyle H.; Langsdorf, Edmond; and Richmond,   (I, J, S)
Robert W.   *Kansas: A Pictorial History.*   Kansas   op
State Historical Society, 1961.   319p.

There goes Kansas, and all Hell can't stop her.

To commemorate one hundred years of Kansas statehood three
native Kansans collaborated to produce this history, comprising a brief
text, maps, and pictures never before collected and organized in book
form. The arrangement is chronological and includes the early explorations through the struggle for statehood. Lives of pioneers are highlighted. Historical society files have made possible this effective history
of the state.

316   Miller, Wilford L., and Larson, Delores.   *Animals of*   (I, J, S)
the Prairie.   Record Printers, 1964.   203p.   op

The uncommon spiny soft-shelled turtle is found in the Missouri
River and its tributaries.

Geographical factors, climate, elevation, and soil characteristics
are considered in this study of North Dakota's past and present wildlife. Early explorers found an abundance of buffalo, elk, moose, black
bears, and grizzlies roaming the prairies. The photographs by Wilford
Miller supplement the illustrations by Delores Larson to help acquaint
the reader with the common birds and animals of the prairie.

317   Moody, Ralph.   *The Dry Divide.*   Illus. by Tran   (J, S)
Mawicke.   Norton, 1963.   230p.

Although I had no right to be bossing, the other fellows seemed willing enough to have me tell them what to do.

Penniless Ralph Moody, kicked off a freight in McCook, Nebraska, on July 4, 1919, joined a motley wheat harvest crew near the Kansas-Nebraska border. Rotten food, a cruel boss, and broken-down equipment seemed insurmountable obstacles, but Ralph was master of the situation. In three months he had persuaded the crew to save the wheat and market it, thereby gaining the respect of the community and acquiring eight teams of horses for himself. This amazing account presents an accurate picture of the life of a harvest crew.

318 Moody, Ralph. *Horse of a Different Color:*   (J, S)
Reminiscences of a Kansas Drover. Norton, 1968.
272p.

In western Kansas anyone living within ten miles is a neighbor.

After a summer with a harvesting crew and a season of hauling Kansas grain, which was detailed in *The Dry Divide*, Ralph Moody decided to invest his small savings, his energy, and his enthusiasm in the livestock business. With backing from the banker, Bones Kennedy, he began trading and shipping mortgaged cattle and hogs in 1919. Later, he joined Bob Wilson in a livestock feeding project. The business was almost wiped out by a blizzard and a flood, but assistance from neighbors and friends allowed recovery. The book provides an authentic picture of the struggles of western farmers in the early 1900s.

319 Muilenburg, Grace, and Swineford, Ada. *Land of*   (S)
the Post Rock. Univ. Press of Kansas, 1975. 207p.

Stone posts . . . shining, like elongated lights on a landscape.

A substitute for timber was essential to early settlers in north-central Kansas, and their use of available limestone is a monument to their resourcefulness. Dugouts and sod houses were replaced by substantial stone buildings, many of which have been preserved. This book provides an excellent guide to the post rock heritage. Information on limestone formation is followed by firsthand accounts of quarrying. Valuable coverage is given to ethnic groups in the region. Numerous maps, illustrations, and photographs, including ten in full color, and a complete index are included.

320 Murray, Stanley Norman. *The Valley Comes of Age.*   (S)
North Dakota Institute for Regional Studies, 1967.
250p.

Because the soil . . . is so productive, the Red River commonly has been termed "The American Nile."

This well-documented history deals with three periods in the development of the Red River Valley. Prior to 1870 a gradual shift in industry from fur trading to farming occurred. From 1870 to 1885 events led to the bonanza boom. From 1885 to 1920 the Red River's agriculture grew in importance. However, this is a social as well as an agricultural history, for the two were inextricably intertwined in the Red River Valley. Well-indexed, this work also has an extensive bibliography.

321   Nebraska State Retired Teachers Assn.   *Telling Tales*   (J, S)
Out of School.   Augstums Print Service, 1976.   199p.

If we live through this, it'll be something to tell our grandchildren!

This collection of reminiscences by retired teachers combines humor, optimism, and at times unpleasant reality as they describe their encounters with blizzards; their problems caused by lack of facilities, materials, and cooperation; and their continuing bouts with rattlesnakes. Endless possibilities exist for comparison with present-day schools, and today's grandchildren will enjoy reading about Nebraska's past as reported by those who lived it.

322   Neihardt, John G.   *The River and I.*   Putnam, 1910.   (S)
325p.   (Paperback ed., Univ. of Nebraska Pr., 1968)   op

I think God wished to teach the beauty of a virile soul fighting its way toward peace—and His precept was the Missouri.

Mammoth dams of the Bureau of Reclamation have tamed the Missouri today, but when John Neihardt and two of his friends descended the river by rowboat from Benton, Montana, to Sioux City, Iowa, in 1908, there were no man-made barriers to their fifty-six day, two thousand-mile journey. Those interested in conservation and ecology could ask for no greater exponent than Neihardt, who confessed to a life-long feeling of awe and reverence for the Missouri and wrote lyrically of his adventures. "To me, it is an epic. And it gave me my first big boy dreams."

323   Nelson, Bruce.   *Land of the Dacotahs.*   Univ. of   (S)
Minnesota Pr., 1946.   354p.   (Paperback ed., Univ.
of Nebraska Pr., 1964)

Of the inexplicable ways of the white man the Indians said, with a chuckle, "The white man looks at his watch to see if it's time to be hungry."

An invigorating, lively style is used as Nelson covers a wide range of topics, including early explorations, the fur trade, Indian wars, the cattle industry, political history, and the development of the Missouri

River basin. Travel, adventure, and history are a part of this appealing record of North Dakota.

324   Nelson, Truman. *The Old Man: John Brown at*   (S)
       Harper's Ferry. Holt, 1973. 304p.   op

> The Old Man arrived at Harper's Ferry on the Fourth of July with a well-matured plan.

The author's purpose in this highly readable account of the raid at Harper's Ferry and its aftermath is to present John Brown as America's greatest revolutionary, not as a fanatic. Brown believed that Northern abolitionists would join him when he took over the arsenal at Harper's Ferry, but instead he was captured the following day and hanged for treason two months later. The events covered begin with "The Coup" and end with "Body in Transit."

325   Neuberger, Richard L. *The Lewis and Clark*   (I)
       Expedition. Illus. by Winold Reiss. (Landmark
       Books) Random, 1951. 179p.

> We must remember that these men had no cameras, not even an old-fashioned kodak with bellows and cloth hood.

This easy-to-understand account of the historic expedition is recorded as it appeared to Sergeant John Ordway, a soldier of the U.S. Army who was ordered to accompany the noted captains to the Western Ocean. The reader is made aware that many common animals were seen for the first time on this journey and many geographic features named. A study of the place-names in one's own state could appropriately follow as a student activity.

326   Nicoll, Bruce Hilton, comp. *Nebraska: A Pictorial*   (I, J, S)
       History. Rev. ed. Univ. of Nebraska Pr., 1975. 240p.
       (Paperback ed., 1975)

> The story of our state is . . . one of optimism and doubt, promise and frustration.

Photographs, maps, paintings, and drawings allow the reader to focus on details often missing from more voluminous Nebraska works. Rural life, development of cities, life of the Indians, improvement of communication, and forms of entertainment are among the topics included. This book would be a fine supplement to books on Nebraska without illustrations; yet it is an important selection in itself.

327   O'Gara, W. H., comp. *In All Its Fury: A History of*   (J, S)
       the Blizzard of January 12, 1888. Union College Pr.,   op
       1967. 343p. (Paperback ed., Doris Jenkins, 1975)

Never in all my experiences have I seen any thing that appeared more like a wild thing from the jungle than did that storm.

Nebraska weather has been a source of frustration to residents since pioneer times. Droughts, tornadoes, floods, and winds have challenged the brave and driven out less courageous individuals. However, perhaps the most savage force is the prairie blizzard. In 1888, an extremely sudden change in the weather turned an ordinary snowstorm into an incredibly violent blizzard which affected a huge area. Personal accounts of the blizzard's survivors reveal that intelligence, courage, and knowledge were needed to deal adequately with the situation. Newspaper stories, excerpts from other books on the blizzard, a list of members of the January 12, 1888 Blizzard Club, photographs, and weather maps are included.

328 O'Kieffe, Charley. *Western Story: The Recollections*   (J, S)
      of Charley O'Kieffe, 1884–1898. (Pioneer Heritage   op
      Series) Univ. of Nebraska Pr., 1960. 224p.
      (Paperback ed., 1974)

   This was a new country and folks had to learn how to look after themselves.

Charley O'Kieffe's newly-widowed mother follows her original plan to take the family to Nebraska and settle on a claim. Thus, most of Charley's life was spent looking after himself and the fatherless family. This detailed description of pioneer life is peppered with Charley's buoyant yet realistic wit. When his conclusions seem inaccurate, footnotes provide correct information. Supplementary notes at the end of the story provide additional details.

329 Olson, James C.   *J. Sterling Morton.*   Univ. of   (S)
      Nebraska Pr., 1942. 451p. (Reprint ed., Nebraska   op
      State Historical Society Foundation, 1972)

   Arbor Day began inauspiciously. It was simply one of a number of efforts to encourage the planting of trees in barren Nebraska.

Despite its ordinary beginnings, Arbor Day helped fulfill one of Julius Sterling Morton's most cherished dreams—to plant enough trees on the barren Nebraska prairie so that soil erosion would be checked and beauty and food provided for settlers. Through his efforts Morton instigated the planting of over a million trees on the first Arbor Day, no small achievement for a young politician who adopted Nebraska as his home. Although his career was varied, his support for the furthering of agriculture never wavered. The text is illustrated with photographs, and a bibliography and index are included.

330   Oyan, Ethel R.   *South Dakota for Young People.*   (I)
Illus. by Sharon Slupe.   University Publishing, 1975.
220p.

> Come to South Dakota. It is the Sunshine State . . . the Coyote State
> . . . the Land of Infinite Variety.

Responding to a request from the South Dakota Superintendent of
Public Instruction, the author introduces young readers to the wonders
and kaleidoscopic beauties of South Dakota. An easily readable text,
pleasing format, and outstanding monochromatic photographs heighten
its appeal. Words and music for "Hail, South Dakota," the state song,
and many easy-to-read maps are also included.

331   Piper, Marion J.   *Dakota Portraits.*   Marion Piper,   (S)
1964.   231p.   op

> Each one must do his part to show that the nation is worthy of its
> good fortune.

This pictorial history of the state was written to inspire pride in
North Dakota. Almost every page has a well-captioned black-and-white
photograph or a painting. The work provides good reference material
on the history of North Dakota and interesting browsing for citizens
of the state.

332   Rich, Everett.   *The Heritage of Kansas: Selected*   (S)
Commentaries of Past Times.   Univ. of Kansas, Pr.,   op
1960.   359p.   (Paperback ed., Flint Hills Book Co.,
1960)

> Kansas always leads but never follows.

An interesting collection of articles, chosen to present a picture of
life in early Kansas, includes selections by Donald Culross Peattie,
Samuel J. Crawford, Kirke Mechem, and many others. Several accounts
are vivid firsthand descriptions of such events as Quantrill's massacre
and the blizzard of 1886. Elizabeth Custer gives an account of a prairie
fire, E. A. Howe writes of a country newspaper, and A. E. Hertzler
describes the role of a country doctor.

333   Richmond, Robert W.   *Kansas: A Land of Contrasts.*   (J, S)
Forum Pr., 1974.   319p.   (Paperback ed., 1977)

> Kansas . . . holds some of the most beautiful scenery in the United
> States.

Although designed primarily as a textbook, this comprehensive
survey of Kansas beginning with early man and ending with the energy
crisis of the 1970s is an invaluable resource. The chronological history

of the state emphasizes personalities and includes many excellent illustrations from the State Historical Society's file. Extensive bibliographies
at the end of each chapter identify many books as well as numerous
articles from *Kansas Historical Collections* and the *Kansas Historical
Quarterly* for further study.

334 Robinson, Elwyn B. *History of North Dakota.* Illus.   (J, S)
by Jack Brodie.   Univ. of Nebraska Pr., 1966.   599p.

   Before the advent of recorded history, the region that was to become
   North Dakota had many changes of climate and consequently many
   human migrations.

The reader is conducted on a chronological journey through North
Dakota's history from prehistoric times through the 1960s. Each chapter is a detailed explanation of the aspects that shaped the state, including "Indians of the Plains and Prairie," "The Thirties: Drought and
Depression," and "The Character of the People." The work is well-
indexed.

335 Rolfsrud, Erling Nicolai. *The Story of North Dakota.*   (J, S)
Lantern Books, 1963.   283p.   op

   "It is fit only for the Indians and the devil," General Sibley decided
   after traveling the parched Dakota prairies in 1863.

Many Americans shared Sibley's opinion, as J. B. Powers discovered when he tried to sell Northern Pacific grant lands. This well-
researched history that reads like a novel is a must for young citizens of
North Dakota. Rolfsrud, well-known North Dakota author, creates a
travelogue from the campfires of the Plains Indians when one hundred
million buffalo roamed the Dakota Territory to the present day. Many
black-and-white photographs encourage browsing.

336 Rounds, Glen. *Buffalo Harvest.*   Holiday, 1952.   (I)
141p.

   None of the Plains tribes planted crops of any kind. Instead, they
   depended on the buffalo for almost everything they needed.

Author/illustrator Glen Rounds describes the northward migration of the great herds, the Indians' preparations for the hunt, the fall
hunting camp, the surrounding of the herd, the butchering, and the
driving of the herds over the bluff at the "Falling Off Place." He item-
izes the products harvested: meat to be dried; hides to be made into
robes and tents; rawhide to be molded into saddle frames, shields, or
war clubs; hoofs to be boiled for glue; horns to be made into spoons
and ladles; and sinews to be made into bowstrings.

337   Rounds, Glen. *The Cowboy Trade.* Holiday, 1972.   (I)
       95p.

> Cowboys . . . liked to think of themselves as men who could ride
> anything with legs on the four corners and hair on the outside.

The cowboy's life is presented realistically rather than as it is
pictured on TV or in "westerns." The day-to-day activities of the cowboy of the Old West include rounding up cattle, fencing, and haying in
summer, chopping ice in winter, and pulling cattle from bogs in spring.
This life, with its demanding routine and monotony, bears little resemblance to that of the screen cowboy riding his horse into a Dodge
City saloon. The author's cartoon-style illustrations add humor and
vitality to the text.

338   Rounds, Glen. *The Prairie Schooners.* Holiday,   (I)
       1968. 95p.

> Grimfaced women pinned up their long skirts and waded about
> seeing to the safe stowing of their possessions.

Life, death, happiness, and sadness are all expertly depicted in this
saga of the westward trail of the prairie schooners. Glen Rounds's illustrations capture both the beauty and the ugliness of the period. Humor
flows through his line drawings of cowhands and tired old trail blazers
fighting the elements. However, troubles and heavy cares were dis-
missed when the fiddles twanged after supper. This entertaining read-
aloud provides useful historical information.

339   Rounds, Glen. *The Treeless Plains.* Holiday, 1967.   (I)
       95p.

> Finding themselves in an almost treeless country . . . the settlers
> were forced to turn to the earth itself for shelter from the violent
> climate.

Glen Rounds was born in a sod house in the South Dakota Badlands and he uses that experience in chronicling the evolution of sod
houses from their dugout antecedents. Offering safety from prairie
fires, they also provided warmth in winter and coolness in summer.
Useful for a unit on shelter, it also provides supplementary reading to
Coatsworth's *The Sod House* (Macmillan, 1967).

340   Rydjord, John. *Indian Place Names.* Univ. of   (J, S)
       Oklahoma Pr., 1968. 380p.

> Out of song and story, poetry and prose, came Indian names.

Kansas Indian place names identify not only the native inhabitants but also eastern groups who attempted to create an Indian frontier in the West. The historical study of place-names is many faceted,

involving geography, literature, folklore, linguistics, and legends. Because there is disagreement among experts regarding the origin, evolution, and meaning of many Indian names, the author included a variety of interpretations. An extensive bibliography is a part of this valuable resource tool.

341 Rydjord, John. *Kansas Place Names.* Univ. of (S)
Oklahoma Pr., 1972. 613p.

> There is probably no state in the Union with such a rich variety of place-names as . . . Kansas.

Historians will value this fascinating book with its extensive index, bibliography, and appendix; but it will also be enjoyed by general readers. Arrangement is topical with many name sources identified, including ethnic groups, nature, the Bible, women, and famous personalities. Two railroad chapters are of special interest. Following each chapter is a map showing locations of towns with names originating from the chapter theme. Readers will be impressed by the amount of research involved.

342 Sallet, Richard. *Russian German Settlements in the* (J, S)
United States. North Dakota Institute for Regional
Studies, 1974. 207p.

> The term "Russian-German" or "German-Russian" is one that may seem puzzling to many Americans because it links two contrasting ethnic groups.

From the 1760s to 1870s German farmers migrated to Russia. In the latter half of the nineteenth century, many emigrated to the North American continent to escape the harsh Russian laws enacted against them. These German farmers settled in many states, but a large number went to the least populated areas of North and South Dakota. Sallet uses many pictures of their early settlements to add interest to his writings.

343 Sandoz, Mari. *These Were the Sioux.* Hastings, (J, S)
1961. 118p. (Paperback ed., Dell, 1971) (Reprint op
ed., Hastings, 1975)

> The Sioux Indians came into my life before I had any preconceived notions about them, or about anyone else.

From her childhood experiences with friendly Indians in northwestern Nebraska, the author learned the meaning of the customs and beliefs of the Oglala Sioux. This small book might be termed a tribute from her heart to a people whom very few whites sought to understand, but whom she respected as wise, responsible, and deeply religious. Here she traces the growth and development of a Sioux child from birth to adulthood, including the views of these Plains Indians on discipline, courting, marriage, family, ownership, and the harmony of all creation. Nine primitive drawings by native artists are included.

344   Schell, Herbert S.   *History of South Dakota.*   3d ed.   (S)
      rev.   Illus. by Jack Brodie.   Univ. of Nebraska Pr.,
      1975.   445p.   (Paperback ed., 1975)

> The history of a state, or even a community, may be regarded as a cross section of the nation at large.

The author, Emeritus Professor of History at the University of South Dakota and acknowledged as the foremost authority on the history of South Dakota, based the first edition of this work in 1961 on more than thirty years of research. His aim was to trace the growth and development of the state from prehistory to the present day, presenting the material chronologically within a topical framework. Particular emphasis is paid to the growth of political institutions during the territorial period, to industrial development, and to the Indian population. Appendixes include a table of counties, the origin of county names, a list of governors, and supplementary readings. The book is well indexed.

345   Scott, Jack Denton.   *Return of the Buffalo.*   Illus. by   (P, I, J)
      Ozzie Sweet.   Putnam, 1976.   64p.

> A single buffalo provided most items that a Plains Indian family needed to live. They used almost everything from the buffalo but its bellow.

In a striking photo-essay, the reader is introduced to the physical features of the plains buffalo which enabled this animal to survive severe droughts and raging blizzards. The dependence of the Plains Indians on the buffalo for survival is explored and contrasted with its wasteful slaughter as the railroads pushed westward. Fortunately, the attempts by the National Buffalo Association to preserve the shaggy animal have been successful, and herds are safe today in a number of national parks and wildlife refuges. The book presents the Plains Indians as "this country's first conservationists."

346   Shank, Margarethe Erdahl.   *The Coffee Train.*   Illus.   (S)
      by Reisie Lonette.   Doubleday, 1953.   285p.   op
      (Reprint ed., Augsburg, 1968)

> At the imperious whistle . . . the people . . . were reminded it was time to pause for afternoon coffee.

The author casts a loving glance backward at her childhood days in North Dakota. Through the eyes of little Mugs, we see a now vanished way of life which was once an important part of America. The many authentic anecdotes of her Norwegian background recall the experiences of other early pioneers.

347   Standing Bear, Luther.   *My People the Sioux.*   (S)
      Houghton, 1928.   288p.   (Reprint ed., Univ. of   op
      Nebraska Pr., 1976)   (Paperback ed., Univ. of
      Nebraska Pr., 1975)

   No one is able to understand the Indian race like an Indian.

   The simple, unpretentious autobiography of an Oglala chief born in 1868 in western South Dakota achieves the purpose of giving white readers a true and authentic account of his people. He describes his boyhood life, his schooling at Carlisle Indian School, and his return to the reservation. However, the book's greatest strength is in its identification of Indian life, customs, and philosophy. Now, fifty years after its publication, Chief Standing Bear's closing question is still appropriate, "Why not give the Indian a chance for full citizenship?"

348   Stewart, Robert E.   *Breeding Birds of North Dakota.*   (S)
      Tri-College Center for Environmental Studies, 1975.
      295p.

   Since the mid-1800's, the breeding bird life in North Dakota has undergone drastic changes.

   Essentially this is an account of 196 bird species which breed in North Dakota. Each is described as are its range, breeding habitat, and nesting characteristics. This carefully documented work also contains an introduction to the environment of North Dakota, its climate, and physiography. Both colored and black-and-white illustrations, as well as many maps, are used to supplement the text.

349   Streeter, Floyd B.   *The Kaw: The Heart of a Nation.*   (S)
      Illus. by Isabel Bate and Harold Black.   (Rivers of   op
      America)   Farrar, 1941.   371p.   (Reprint ed., Arno,
      1975)

   The valley of the Kaw and its tributaries is a vast tapestry.

   The Kaw valley was prominent in early Kansas history as the Indians and pioneers took advantage of the river in establishing their homes and way of life. This highly readable book, from the series edited by Stephen Vincent Benét and Carl Carmer, records the "Bloody Kansas" period, the Kansas cowtown era, and the growth of an agricultural empire. One chapter, "Soldiers of the Pen," identifies Kansas authors. An excellent bibliography and index are included.

111

350 Tallent, Annie D. *The Black Hills; or, The Last*   (S)
Hunting Ground of the Dakotahs. Nixon-Jones   op
Printing, 1899. 713p. (Reprint ed., Brevet Pr., 1974)

Important events . . . have transpired in the Black Hills during . . . twenty-three years of history.

The author, the first white woman in the Black Hills, wrote this pioneer history hoping that the record of those "in the thick of the fray" would be preserved for succeeding generations "in plain, homely diction." She intended that it be a complete history from 1874 to 1899, a record of the struggles between the early settlers and the Dakotah tribes, culminating in the defeat of the Indians and the opening of the land to settlement by the whites. The book has reference value as original source material.

351 Tweton, D. Jerome, and Rylance, Daniel F. *The*   (S)
Years of Despair, North Dakota in the Depression.   op
Oxcart Pr., 1973. 34p.

I wish I had some really good news about our state to communicate.

The quotation was written by Dr. Gillette of the University of North Dakota, the "father of rural sociology," in 1934. During the troubled years of the 1930s, North Dakotans faced ruin from wind, drought, grasshoppers, and the nation's depressed economy. The record of those years of despair is concerned with both the economic and political implications. It is followed by eighty pages of photographs of North Dakota during the depression years.

352 Unrau, William E. *The Kansa Indians: A History of*   (S)
the Wind People, 1673–1873. (The Civilization of
the American Indian) Univ. of Oklahoma Pr., 1971.
244p.

But we like this place and want to stay.

This extensive work traces an important and sad chapter in the history of the Indians in America. Customs are explained to illustrate the impossibility of the tribe's changing its economy from hunting and trapping to agriculture. The Kansa, who had little desire for tilling the soil, were not only exploited by the whites, they were attacked by stronger tribes, as well. They also suffered severely from diseases, especially smallpox, introduced by the white newcomers. This tragic account is well-indexed.

353 Vandergriff, James H. *The Indians of Kansas.*   (I, J, S)
Emporia State Pr., 1973. 199p.   op

The customs of each tribe vary a great deal.

Numerous requests for material no longer in print prompted this unbiased record of the Indians of Kansas which appeared originally in a periodical, *Heritage of Kansas*. Firsthand accounts aid in presenting the hope and despair of the six tribes. The book appropriately begins with two beautiful Indian legends and closes with "Buffalo: Lord of the Plains," for the destruction of the buffalo by the whites signaled the end of the Plains Indian culture. Each section of the book may be used independently.

354   Vandiver, Frank E.   *John J. Pershing and the Anatomy*   (S)
      of Leadership.   (Harmon Memorial Lectures)   United   op
      States Air Force Academy, 1963.   21p.

  "Pershing's years in Lincoln may have been among the most influential in his life."

In a lecture delivered to the Air Force Academy Cadet Wing, Dr. Vandiver terms General Pershing as "a man much maligned and mostly misunderstood." Because Pershing possessed character, wit, and human understanding, he learned from every experience. In 1891 his love for ideas and books made him quickly accept an opportunity to become Professor of Military Tactics at the University of Nebraska. In his four-year stay he worked with the famed Pershing Rifles, made radical changes in the university cadet corps, and was admitted to the bar. The author deals briefly with Pershing's military career and only a small portion of the book is devoted to his Lincoln assignment.

355   Veglahn, Nancy.   *Getting to Know the Missouri River.*   (I)
      Illus. by William K. Plummer.   (Getting to Know
      Books)   Coward, 1972.   71p.

  The Missouri was "too thick to drink, too thin to plow."

Among the longest rivers in the western hemisphere and one of the most difficult rivers in the world to navigate, the Big Muddy constantly carves new channels through the earth. Father Marquette was the first white man to view it, Lewis and Clark explored its length, Manuel Lisa and John Colter floated furs along its route to St. Louis, and Carl Bodmer and George Catlin painted its wild and beautiful landscapes. Today dams that power great electrical generators have tamed its floods and changed its behavior. A chronology of important dates and an index are included.

356   Veglahn, Nancy.   *South Dakota.*   (States of the   (J)
      Nation)   Coward, 1970.   125p.   op

  The Missouri river . . . goes . . . from old to new, and the state through which it goes is moving too.

One may grasp the scope of this book through such chapter headings as "The River"; "Pheasants and Farms"; "Fossils, Cliffs and Caves"; "The Reservations"; and "The People." As with other books in this series, there is a profile of important facts about products, government, and moments in state history; a pronunciation guide to place-names; and a carefully prepared index. This work was prepared in consultation with the director of curriculum for the South Dakota Department of Public Instruction.

357 Vestal, Stanley. *The Missouri.* Illus. by Getlar Smith. (S)
(The Rivers of America) Farrar, 1945. 368p. op
(Paperback ed., Univ. of Nebraska Pr., 1964)

> The Missouri River is a story in itself . . . an heroic poem, an epic.

Telling the history of the Missouri in one volume is comparable to packing an elephant into a sardine can, according to the author. He succeeded in covering the 2,500 miles of his subject's history by following it from its mouth to its source and packing the account with fact and gossipy legend. The book is arranged in three sections: "Highway," "Boundary," and "Outpost." As highway, the Missouri led to the snowy peaks of the Rockies; as boundary, it divided two kinds of climate, two cultures, two topographies; as outpost, it served as a base of operations for the winning of the West. This animated, highly readable book is footnoted and includes a bibliography and an index.

358 Vestal, Stanley. *Queen of the Cowtowns: Dodge City.* (S)
Harper, 1952. 285p. (Paperback ed., Univ. of op
Nebraska Pr., 1972)

> For nearly fifteen years Dodge City was the wildest town in the West.

Stanley Vestal has done extensive research and writing on the West. Not a full history of Dodge City, this is a collection of anecdotes, episodes, and incidents that portray the "Wickedest Little City in America, 1872–1886." In it authorities and tombstone epitaphs are quoted and courthouse records used to create what has been called a "dime novel and a document in our social history." Boot Hill, the vigilantes, gamblers, horse thieves, train robbers, and marshalls are among its topics.

359 Vines, Peg, ed. *Kansas: Its Power and Its Glory.* (J, S)
John R. Peach, 1966. 312p. (Available from Mrs. op
John R. Peach).

> The Flint Hills are changeless and unchanging.

The inclusion of hard-to-locate information and material makes this book particularly valuable to a Kansas collection. A large part of the book is devoted to a city index with full-page coverage on many towns, as well as statistics concerning others. Names of city newspapers are provided. Several signed articles are written by such experts as James A. McCain, former president of Kansas State University, who wrote "Prospects Unlimited for Kansas Wheat." The coverage of Kansas authors, several articles on business in the state, and excellent color and black-and-white photographs are important features.

360 Webb, Bernice Larson. *The Basketball Man.* Univ.   (S)
     Press of Kansas, 1973. 381p.
     They did not know that the basketball shots fired that morning would be "heard around the world."

In 1891 James Naismith presented to one of his classes an idea which was to give pleasure to thousands in ensuing years. Assigned to develop an indoor game for bad weather, he developed the peach basket game with its thirteen rules and nine players. Detailed information on Naismith's years at Kansas University are part of the record of the growth of basketball. Naismith's greatest moment came at the Berlin Olympics in 1936 as the flag of each nation represented was dipped in his honor.

361 Welsch, Roger L. *Sod Walls: The Story of the*   (I, J, S)
     Nebraska Sod House. Purcell's, 1968. 208p.   op
     The wagon load of "Nebraska marble," as the wags often called it, was hauled from the low ground, where the best wild grasses were to be found, to the home site.

Based on extensive research, this detailed study of sod house construction also examines the lives of Nebraska pioneers whose problems included harsh weather conditions, lack of fuel, food shortages, loneliness, and other privations. Although pioneer life was difficult, it did have its diversions, such as square dancing. Photographs of Nebraska soddies enhance the usefulness of this valuable source.

362 Whittemore, Margaret. *Historic Kansas: A*   (I, J, S)
     Centenary Sketchbook. Univ. of Kansas Pr., 1954.   op
     223p. (Paperback ed., Flint Hills Book Co., 1954)
     No outsider should think of it as a state to drive through without looking to the right or left.

Numerous visits were made by the author to the historic landmarks which she sketched and organized into this beautiful book that could serve as a guide for visitors as well as native Kansans. The many outstanding illustrations are complemented by the brief text which traces Kansas history from prehistoric times. The author's hope is that readers of the book may become interested and involved in the preservation of landmarks.

363 Williams, Mary Ann Barnes. *Origins of North Dakota*   (J, S)
     Place Names. Bismarck Tribune, 1966. 345p.

> In some instances it seems that time and change have put a silent seal on the record of many worthy pioneers and the places they established.

What's in a name? Much of North Dakota's history may be found in this fascinating account of the derivation and background of the state's place-names. The famous people such as Bismarck, McKenzie, and Pierre Bottineau; the first white child born in North Dakota; the distinctive places with descriptive names such as Grassy Butte, Lone Tree, and Golden Valley; and the Indian names such as Mandaree and Neche all speak of the varied and interesting history of the state. Many readers will be interested in finding out how the places they know came to be named.

364 Wills, Bernt Lloyd. *North Dakota: Geography and*   (I)
     Early History. Univ. of North Dakota Pr., 1967. 277p.   op

> The core of the study is man and land—the North Dakotan in time and space.

This textbook evolved in response to a need for a geography and early history of North Dakota for fourth-grade students. In it Wills strives to instill in his readers appreciation and respect for the state and to inspire them to good citizenship. Photographs and maps elucidate the text. The comprehensive index is helpful.

365 Wills, Bernt Lloyd. *North Dakota: The Northern*   (J, S)
     Prairie State. Edwards Brothers, 1963. 318p.   op

> This is an account of the geography of a northern prairie state.

A native North Dakotan writes of a state he truly appreciates. His selection of content material is designed to inform and prepare the reader to adapt successfully to that state's environment. The non-technical treatment enhances the book's readability. An index is appended.

366 Writers' Program. *Kansas: A Guide to the Sunflower*   (I, J, S)
     State. (American Guide) Hastings, 1939. 538p.   op
     (Reprint ed., Somerset Publishers, 1975)

> Kansas has weathered many calamities and earned its motto, "To the stars through difficulties."

This welcome reprint of Kansas's first guidebook, prepared by the Federal Writers' Project, is a useful historical source. Thirteen tours covering all sections of the state give pertinent facts about towns along each tour route. Sectional maps identify places of interest, and a detailed chronology lists significant dates. Numerous pictures and an extensive index are included.

367   Wyman, Walker D.   *Nothing but Prairie and Sky:*   (S)
      Life on the Dakota Range in the Early Days.   op
      (Western Frontier Library) Univ. of Oklahoma Pr.,
      1954.   217p.   (Reprint ed., 1970)

   After a summer herding horses in South Dakota a man can get about as much prairie and sky as he can stand.

Bruce Sibert's longhand reminiscences, begun when he was seventy-seven years of age, provided the basis for this amalgam of South Dakota social history, folklore, and tall tales. In 1890 Sibert, then a young man of twenty-two, went from Mount Pleasant, Iowa, to the Black Hills in search of his fortune. After working on the railroad, carrying a hod at Hot Springs, and running cattle, he settled on a career of horse ranching. Range life, customs, rustlers, rattlers, blizzards, broncos, Indians, and frontier life in Pierre are included among his memories of what life was like at the turn of the century. All are described in the salty speech of a western cowboy.

368   Zornow, William Frank.   *Kansas: A History of the*   (S)
      Jayhawk State.   Univ. of Oklahoma Pr., 1957.   417p.   op
      (Reprint ed., 1971)

   Its greatest cash receipts from farm marketing have come from livestock and livestock products.

Recognized as one of the most reliable sources on the subject, this history has been used extensively by other authors as a secondary source. Coverage begins with the early Spanish explorers and ends with preparations for the Kansas centennial observance. Six chapters on politics from 1861 to 1956 are particularly valuable. Well-chosen illustrations appear frequently. A comprehensive bibliography and an extensive index are appended.

STATE LISTS

The State Lists provide for each state covered an author-title key, arranged by category, to the books listed in the Annotated Bibliography, indicating by number their location therein. If a book pertains to more than one state, it appears in the listing for each. Reading level is indicated in parentheses following each title.

KANSAS

FICTION

7   Bliss, Ronald G. *Indian Softball Summer or Kickapoos Never Say Good-bye* (I)

15   Calhoun, Mary. *High Wind for Kansas.* (P, I)

20   Chandler, Edna Walker. *Chaff in the Wind.* (S)

22   Coatsworth, Elizabeth. *The Sod House.* (P, I)

23   Constant, Alberta Wilson. *Those Miller Girls.* (I, J)

31   Erdman, Loula Grace. *Many a Voyage.* (S)

32   Fernald, Helen Clark. *Plow the Dew Under.* (J, S)

34   Fisher, Aileen. *Homestead of the Free.* (I, J)

37   Hager, Jean. *The Whispering House.* (I)

45   Holling, Holling C. *Tree in the Trail.* (I, J)

55   Johnson, Norma. *What Would We See?* (P)

56   Keith, Harold. *The Bluejay Boarders.* (I)

57   Laman, Russell. *Manifest Destiny.* (S)

58   Lane, Neola Tracy. *Grasshopper Year.* (I)

62   Le Grand. *Cats for Kansas.* (P)

68   Mohler, Marjorie M. *Brave Heritage.* (I, J)

71   Parks, Gordon. *The Learning Tree.* (J, S)

94   Taylor, Ross McLaury. *We Were There on the Chisholm Trail.* (I, J)

95 _____ *We Were There on the Santa Fe Trail.* (I, J)
96 Tomerlin, John. *The Fledgling.* (J, S)
97 Trump, Fred. *Uphill into the Sun.* (S)
98 Turnbull, Roderick. *More Maple Hill Stories.* (I, J, S)
100 Wellman, Manly Wade. *Frontier Reporter.* (J, S)
103 Wilder, Laura Ingalls. *Little House on the Prairie.* (I, J, S)
107 Williams, Jeanne. *Coyote Winter.* (I, J)
108 _____ *Freedom Trail.* (J)
109 _____ *Oh, Susanna!* (J, S)
110 _____ *Winter Wheat.* (I, J)
112 Wyatt, Geraldine. *Buffalo Gold.* (I, J)

FOLKTALES

115 Bierhorst, John, ed. *The Ring in the Prairie: A Shawnee Legend.* (I, J)
119 Marriott, Alice, and Rachlin, Carol K. *Plains Indian Mythology.* (I, J)
121 Sackett, S. J., and Koch, William E. *Kansas Folklore.* (I, J, S)
122 Welsch, Roger. *Shingling the Fog and Other Plains Lies.* (J, S)

POETRY, DRAMA, MUSIC

124 Benét, Stephen Vincent. *John Brown's Body.* (S)
127 Cutler, Bruce. *A West Wind Rises.* (S)
131 Kliewer, Warren, and Solomon, Stanley J., eds. *Kansas Renaissance.* (S)

BIOGRAPHY AND PERSONAL ACCOUNTS

135 Alexander, Lloyd. *Border Hawk: August Bondi.* (I, J)
136 Anderson, Anita M., and Regli, Adolph. *Alec Majors, Trail Boss.* (P, I)
138 Aulaire, Ingri d' and Edgar Parin d'. *Buffalo Bill.* (P, I)
139 Beckhard, Arthur J. *The Story of Dwight D. Eisenhower.* (J, S)
150 De Leeuw, Adele. *The Story of Amelia Earhart.* (I, J)
170 Hatch, Alden. *Young Ike.* (P, I)
173 Hertzler, Arthur. *Horse and Buggy Doctor.* (S)
175 Holbrook, Stewart H. *Wyatt Earp, U.S. Marshal.* (I, J)
176 Howe, Jane Moore. *Amelia Earhart: Kansas Girl.* (P, I)

178 Iger, Eve Marie. *John Brown: His Soul Goes Marching On.* (J, S)

190 Lovelace, Delos W. *"Ike" Eisenhower: Statesman and Soldier of Peace.* (I, J)

197 Nelson, Cordner. *The Jim Ryun Story.* (I, J, S)

199 Nolan, Jeannette Covert. *John Brown.* (I, J)

204 Parks, Gordon. *A Choice of Weapons.* (J, S)

230 Werenstein, Irving. *Marshall without a Gun, Tom Smith.* (J, S)

231 White, William Allen. *The Autobiography of William Allen White.* (S)

OTHER INFORMATIONAL BOOKS

237 Adams, Samuel Hopkins. *The Santa Fe Trail.* (I, J)

239 Alston, Eugenia. *Come Visit a Prairie Dog Town.* (P)

240 Bailey, Bernadine. *Picture Book of Kansas.* (I)

250 Branch, Edward Douglas. *The Hunting of the Buffalo.* (J, S)

257 Carpenter, Allan. *Kansas.* (I)

261 Coe, Edith C. *Hertzler Heritage.* (S)

262 Collins, Joseph T. *Amphibians and Reptiles in Kansas.* (I, J, S)

263 Costello, David F. *The World of the Prairie Dog.* (I, J, S)

265 Cross, Frank B., and Collins, Joseph T. *Fishes in Kansas.* (J, S)

266 Davis, Kenneth S. *Kansas: A Bicentennial History.* (S)

271 Duffus, Robert Luther. *The Santa Fe Trail.* (S)

272 Engel, Lorenz. *Among the Plains Indians.* (I, J, S)

278 Gladstone, T. H. *The Englishman in Kansas.* (S)

280 Goodrum, Charles. *I'll Trade You an Elk.* (J, S)

284 Hayden, Ruth Kelley. *The Time That Was.* (J, S)

285 Heilman, Grant, ed. *Farm Town: A Memoir of the 1930's* (I, J, S)

287 Howes, Charles. *This Place Called Kansas.* (J, S)

288 Humble, Emma. *The Jayhawker Book.* (P)

291 Ise, John. *Sod and Stubble.* (J, S)

292 Isely, Bliss. *Early Days in Kansas.* (P, I)

297 Kaufman, Edna Ramseyer. *Melting Pot of Mennonite Cookery 1874–1974.* (S)

302 Lauber, Patricia. *Dust Bowl: The Story of Man on the Great Plains.* (I, J)

304 Lindquist, Emory. *Bethany in Kansas: The History of a College.* (S)

305 Long, R. W. *Wichita Century.* (J, S)

306 Lyle, Wes, and Fisher, James. *Kansas Impressions.* (I, J, S)

313 Miller, Nyle H. *Kansas—The 34th Star.* (I, J, S)
314 Miller, Nyle H., and Snell, Joseph W. *Great Gunfighters of the Kansas Cowtowns, 1867–1886.* (J, S)
315 Miller, Nyle H.; Langsdorf, Edmond; and Richmond, Robert W. *Kansas: A Pictorial History.* (I, J, S)
318 Moody, Ralph. *Horse of a Different Color: Reminiscences of a Kansas Drover.* (J, S)
319 Muilenburg, Grace, and Swineford, Ada. *Land of the Post Rock.* (S)
324 Nelson, Truman. *The Old Man: John Brown at Harper's Ferry.* (S)
332 Rich, Everett. *The Heritage of Kansas: Selected Commentaries on Past Times.* (S)
333 Richmond, Robert W. *Kansas: A Land of Contrasts.* (J, S)
338 Rounds, Glen. *The Prairie Schooners.* (I)
340 Rydjord, John. *Indian Place Names.* (J, S)
341 _____ *Kansas Place Names.* (S)
349 Streeter, Floyd B. *The Kaw: The Heart of a Nation.* (S)
352 Unrau, William E. *The Kansa Indians: A History of the Wind People, 1673–1873.* (S)
353 Vandergriff, James H. *The Indians of Kansas.* (I, J, S)
358 Vestal, Stanley. *Queen of the Cowtowns: Dodge City.* (S)
359 Vines, Peg, ed. *Kansas: Its Power and Its Glory.* (J, S)
360 Webb, Bernice Larson. *The Basketball Man.* (S)
362 Whittemore, Margaret. *Historic Kansas: A Centenary Sketchbook.* (I, J, S)
366 Writers' Program. *Kansas: A Guide to the Sunflower State.* (I, J, S)
368 Zornow, William Frank. *Kansas: A History of the Jayhawk State.* (S)

NEBRASKA

FICTION

1 Aldrich, Bess Streeter. *Journey into Christmas and Other Stories.* (J, S)
2 _____ *A Lantern in Her Hand.* (J, S)
3 _____ *The Rim of the Prairie.* (S)
5 Barker, Mary Libal. *Milenka's Happy Summer.* (I)
8 Bonham, Barbara. *Challenge of the Prairie.* (I, J)
9 Bothwell, Jean. *Peter Holt, P. K.* (I)
10 _____ *Tree House at Seven Oaks: A Story of the Flat Water Country in 1853.* (J)
12 Brown, Marion Marsh. *Frontier Beacon.* (J)

122

13 _____ *Marnie.* (J)
14 _____ *Prairie Teacher.* (J, S)
17 Cather, Willa. *My Ántonia.* (J, S)
18 _____ *O Pioneers!* (S)
19 _____ *Obscure Destinies.* (S)
27 Davis, Clyde Brion. *Nebraska Coast.* (S)
30 Dick, Trella Lamson. *Tornado Jones.* (I)
38 Hays, Wilma Pitchford. *The Apricot Tree.* (J, S)
39 _____ *Little Lone Coyote.* (P, I)
46 Hosford, Jessie. *An Awful Name to Live Up to.* (I)
47 _____ *You Bet Your Boots I Can.* (J, S)
53 Jackson, Charles Tenney. *The Buffalo Wallow: A Prairie Boy-hood.* (J)
54 John, Alvin. *The Battle of the Wild Turkey and Other Tales.* (J, S)
61 Laughlin, Florence. *The Seventh Cousin.* (I)
73 Reilly, Robert T. *Massacre at Ash Hollow.* (J, S)
74 Rock, Gail. *Addie and the King of Hearts.* (I, J)
75 _____ *The Thanksgiving Treasure.* (P, I)
82 Sandoz, Mari. *Miss Morissa.* (S)
83 _____ *Sandhill Sundays and Other Recollections.* (J, S)
84 _____ *The Story Catcher.* (I)
85 _____ *Winter Thunder.* (I, J)
111 Winther, Sophus Keith. *Take All to Nebraska.* (S)
113 Yates, Elizabeth. *Carolina's Courage.* (P, I)

FOLKTALES

114 Beath, Paul K., comp. *Febold Feboldson: Tall Tales from the Great Plains.* (J, S)
120 Pound, Louise. *Nebraska Folklore.* (J, S)
123 Welsch, Roger L., comp. *A Treasury of Nebraska Pioneer Folklore.* (J, S)

POETRY, DRAMA, MUSIC

126 Cleary, Kate McPhelim. *The Nebraska of Kate McPhelim Cleary.* (J, S)
130 Jaffe, Dan. *Dan Freeman.* (S)

BIOGRAPHY AND PERSONAL ACCOUNTS

142 Brown, Marion Marsh, and Crone, Ruth. *Willa Cather: The Woman and Her Works.* (J, S)

144 Chrisman, Berna Hunter. *When You and I Were Young, Nebraska!* (J, S)

145 Clark, Rose B. *My Nebraska Childhood: The Ought-to-Biography of an Octogenarian.* (I, J, S)

146 Cook, Harold J. *Tales of the 04 Ranch.* (J, S)

154 Edwards, Leta M. *Sauce for the Geese: The Story of a Nebraska Farm.* (J, S)

158 Filley, H. Clyde. *Every Day Was New: The Story of the Growth of Nebraska.* (S)

159 Franchere, Ruth. *Willa: The Story of Willa Cather's Growing Up.* (I, J)

162 Garst, Shannon. *Crazy Horse, Great Warrior of the Sioux.* (I, J)

166 Glad, Paul W. *The Trumpet Soundeth: William Jennings Bryan and His Democracy, 1896–1912.* (S)

167 Governor's Commission on the Status of Women. *Nebraska Women through the Years, 1867–1967.* (I, J, S)

168 Green, Norma Kidd. *Iron Eye's Family: The Children of Joseph La Flesche.* (S)

177 Hutton, Harold. *Doc Middleton: Life and Legends of the Notorious Plains Outlaw.* (S)

180 Johnson, John R. *Representative Nebraskans.* (J, S)

184 Kauffman, Bernice, comp. *Nebraska Centennial Literary Map and Guide to Nebraska Authors.* (I, J, S)

185 Kelley, Peggy A. Volzke. *Women of Nebraska Hall of Fame.* (I, J, S)

186 King, James T. *War Eagle: A Life of General Eugene A. Carr.* (S)

187 Kosner, Alice. *The Voice of the People: William Jennings Bryan.* (J, S)

188 Kyner, James H. *End of Track.* (J, S)

189 Levine, Lawrence W. *Defender of the Faith: William Jennings Bryan: The Last Decade, 1915–1925.* (S)

191 Lowitt, Richard. *George W. Norris: The Making of a Progressive, 1881–1912.* (S)

192 McKelvie, Martha. *Sandhills Essie.* (S)

193 Meadowcroft, Enid LaMonte. *Crazy Horse: Sioux Warrior.* (P)

196 Neihardt, John G. *All Is but a Beginning.* (J, S)

198 Nicoll, Bruce H., and Keller, Ken R. *Sam McKelvie: Son of the Soil.* (J, S)

200 Norris, George W. *Fighting Liberal.* (S)

201 North, Luther. *Man of the Plains: Recollections of Luther North, 1856–1882.* (S)
202 O'Connell, Frank. *Farewell to the Farm.* (S)
210 Russell, Don. *The Lives and Legends of Buffalo Bill.* (S)
212 Sandoz, Mari. *Old Jules.* (S)
213 Sanford, Mollie Dorsey. *Mollie.* (S)
214 Sergeant, Elizabeth Shepley. *Willa Cather: A Memoir.* (S)
218 Slote, Bernice. *Willa Cather.* (I, J, S)
219 Snyder, Albert B., and Yost, Nellie Snyder. *Pinnacle Jake.* (S)
220 Snyder, Grace. *No Time on My Hands.* (J, S)
221 Stith, Forrest M. *Sunrises and Sunsets for Freedom.* (J, S)
235 Yost, Nellie Snyder, ed. *Boss Cowman: The Recollections of Ed Lemmon, 1857–1946.* (J, S)

OTHER INFORMATIONAL BOOKS

238 Alberts, Francis Jacobs, ed. *Sod House Memories,* vols. 1–3. (J, S)
241 Bailey, Bernadine. *Picture Book of Nebraska.* (I)
244 Barns, Cass Grove. *The Sod House.* (J, S)
254 *Broken Hoops and Plains People.* (J, S)
264 Crabb, Richard. *Empire on the Platte.* (S)
267 Dick, Everett. *Sod-House Frontier, 1854–1890.* (J, S)
274 Faulkner, Virginia, comp. *Roundup: A Nebraska Reader.* (J, S)
275 Fisher, Aileen. *Arbor Day.* (P, I)
276 Fitzpatrick, Lilian L. *Nebraska Place-Names.* (I, J, S)
281 Graber, Kay, comp. *Nebraska Pioneer Cookbook.* (I, J, S)
286 Horn, Huston. *The Pioneers.* (J, S)
290 Hyde, George. *Red Cloud's Folk: A History of the Oglala Sioux Indians.* (S)
301 La Flesche, Francis. *The Middle Five.* (I, J)
308 McKee, James L., and Duerschner, Arthur. *Lincoln: A Photographic History.* (I, J, S)
309 McKeown, Martha Ferguson. *Them Was the Days.* (J, S)
312 Mattes, Merrill J. *The Great Platte River Road.* (S)
317 Moody, Ralph. *The Dry Divide.* (J, S)
321 Nebraska State Retired Teachers Assn. *Telling Tales Out of School.* (J, S)
326 Nicoll, Bruce Hilton, comp. *Nebraska: A Pictorial History.* (I, J, S)
327 O'Gara, W. H., comp. *In All Its Fury: A History of the Blizzard of January 12, 1888.* (J, S)

328 O'Kieffe, Charley. *Western Story: The Recollections of Charley O'Kieffe, 1884–1898.* (J, S)
329 Olson, James C. *J. Sterling Morton.* (S)
354 Vandiver, Frank E. *John J. Pershing and the Anatomy of Leadership.* (S)
357 Vestal, Stanley. *The Missouri.* (S)
361 Welsch, Roger L. *Sod Walls: The Story of the Nebraska Sod House.* (I, J, S)

NORTH DAKOTA

FICTION

29 DeRegniers, Beatrice Schenk. *The Snow Party.* (P)
36 Goble, Paul and Dorothy. *Lone Bull's Horse Raid.* (I)
41 Hoffine, Lyla. *Carol Blue Wing, What Is Your Pleasure?* (J, S)
42 ———— *The Eagle Feather Prize.* (I)
43 ———— *Jennie's Mandan Bowl.* (I)
44 ———— *Running Elk.* (I)
48 Hubbard, Margaret Ann. *The Trouble on Shake-Rag Creek.* (I)
49 Hudson, Lois Phillips. *The Bones of Plenty.* (S)
50 ———— *Reapers of the Dust: A Prairie Chronicle.* (S)
63 Lenski, Lois. *Little Sioux Girl.* (I)
69 Murphy, Robert. *Wild Geese Calling.* (I)
72 Reese, John Henry. *Big Mutt.* (I, J)
76 Rolfsrud, Erling Nicolai. *Boy from Johnny Butte.* (I)
77 ———— *Gopher Tails for Papa.* (I)
78 ———— *The Tiger-Lily Years.* (I, J, S)
89 Sypher, Lucy Johnston. *Cousins and Circuses.* (I)
90 ———— *The Edge of Nowhere.* (I)
91 ———— *The Spell of the Northern Lights.* (I)
92 ———— *The Turnabout Year.* (I, J)

POETRY, DRAMA, MUSIC

128 Foley, James W. *Foley's Poems.* (P, I, J, S)

BIOGRAPHY AND PERSONAL ACCOUNTS

141 Blackorby, Edward C. *Prairie Rebel: The Public Life of William Lemke.* (S)
143 Chandler, Edna Walker, and Willoughby, Barrett. *Pioneer of Alaska Skies: The Story of Ben Eielson.* (I)

147 Coombs, Charles. *Alaska Bush Pilot.* (I)
148 Custer, Elizabeth B. *"Boots and Saddles"; or, Life in Dakota with General Custer.* (S)
149 Custer, George Armstrong. *My Life on the Plains, or, Personal Experiences with Indians.* (S)
152 Dresden, Donald. *The Marquis de Morès: Emperor of the Bad Lands.* (S)
153 Eastman, Charles A. *Indian Boyhood.* (J, S)
155 Farnsworth, Frances Joyce. *Winged Moccasins: The Story of Sacajawea.* (J)
160 Frazier, Neta Lohnes. *Sacajawea: The Girl Nobody Knows.* (J)
165 Geelan, Agnes. *The Dakota Maverick: The Political Life of William Langer, Also Known as "Wild Bill" Langer.* (S)
169 Harrington, Lyn. *The Luck of the La Vérendryes.* (I, J)
172 Herron, Edward A. *Wings over Alaska: The Story of Carl Ben Eielson.* (I, J)
182 Karolevitz, Robert F. *"E. G.," Inventor by Necessity: The Story of E. G. Melroe and the Melroe Company.* (J, S)
195 Mohberg, Nora. *The Straddlebug.* (J, S)
203 O'Connor, Richard. *Sitting Bull: War Chief of the Sioux.* (I, J)
206 Raaen, Aagot. *Measure of My Days.* (J, S)
208 Rolfsrud, Erling Nicolai. *Extraordinary North Dakotans.* (I, J, S)
209 _____ *Lanterns over the Prairies,* books 1 & 2. (I, J)
215 Sevareid, Eric. *Not So Wild a Dream.* (S)
216 Seymour, Flora Warren. *Bird Girl: Sacagawea.* (I)
217 Slaughter, Linda Warfel. *Linda W. Slaughter's Fortress to Farm, or Twenty-three Years on the Frontier.* (J, S)
222 Syme, Ronald. *The Story of Pierre de la Verendrye, Fur Trader of the North.* (I)
223 Thompson, Era Bell. *American Daughter.* (J, S)
224 Tweton, D. Jerome. *The Marquis de Morès, Dakota Capitalist, French Nationalist.* (S)
227 Vestal, Stanley. *Sitting Bull, Champion of the Sioux.* (S)
229 Welk, Lawrence, and McGeehan, Bernice. *Wunnerful, Wunnerful: The Autobiography of Lawrence Welk.* (S)
233 Woodward, Mary Dodge. *The Checkered Years.* (J, S)

OTHER INFORMATIONAL BOOKS

242 Bailey, Bernadine. *Picture Book of North Dakota.* (I)
249 Bleeker, Sonia. *The Sioux Indians: Hunters and Warriors of the Plains.* (I, J)

251 Brand, Wayne L., and Hector, James G., eds. *North Dakota Decision Makers.* (I, J, S)
252 *Brevet's North Dakota Historical Markers and Sites.* (I, J)
258 Carpenter, Allan. *North Dakota.* (I)
260 Clark, Champ. *The Badlands.* (J, S)
268 Dietrich, Irvine T., and Hove, John, eds. *Conservation of Natural Resources in North Dakota.* (J, S)
269 Drache, Hiram M. *The Challenge of the Prairie: Life and Times of Red River Pioneers.* (S)
270 _____ *The Day of the Bonanza.* (S)
273 Erdoes, Richard. *The Sun Dance People: The Plains Indians, Their Past and Present.* (J, S)
282 Greenwood, Annie S. *North Dakota, Frontier of Opportunity.* (J, S)
283 Grinnell, George Bird. *When Buffalo Ran.* (J, S)
289 Hunter, William C. *Beacon across the Prairie: North Dakota's Land-Grant College.* (S)
293 Israel, Marion. *Dakotas.* (P, I)
298 Kazeck, Melvin E. *North Dakota: A Human and Economic Geography.* (S)
316 Miller, Wilford L., and Larson, Delores. *Animals of the Prairie.* (I, J, S)
320 Murray, Stanley Norman. *The Valley Comes of Age.* (S)
323 Nelson, Bruce. *Land of the Dacotahs.* (S)
331 Piper, Marion J. *Dakota Portraits.* (S)
334 Robinson, Elwyn B. *History of North Dakota.* (J, S)
335 Rolfsrud, Erling Nicolai. *The Story of North Dakota.* (J, S)
342 Sallet, Richard. *Russian German Settlements in the United States.* (J, S)
343 Sandoz, Mari. *These Were the Sioux.* (J, S)
346 Shank, Margarethe Erdahl. *The Coffee Train.* (S)
348 Stewart, Robert E. *Breeding Birds of North Dakota.* (S)
351 Tweton, D. Jerome, and Rylance, Daniel F. *The Years of Despair, North Dakota in the Depression.* (S)
363 Williams, Mary Ann Barnes. *Origins of North Dakota Place Names.* (J, S)
364 Wills, Bernt Lloyd. *North Dakota: Geography and Early History.* (I)
365 _____ *North Dakota: The Northern Prairie State.* (J, S)

SOUTH DAKOTA

FICTION

4 Annixter, Jane and Paul. *Buffalo Chief.* (I, J)

6 Benchley, Nathaniel. *Only Earth and Sky Last Forever.* (J)
11 Breneman, Mary Worthy. *The Land They Possessed.* (S)
16 Carlson, Natalie Savage. *The Tomahawk Family.* (P, I)
21 Cleaver, Vera and Bill. *Dust of the Earth.* (J)
24 Coon, Martha Sutherland. *Georgie's Capital.* (I)
25 Dahl, Borghild. *Karen.* (J)
26 ———— *This Precious Year.* (J)
28 DeLeeuw, Adele Louise. *Blue Ribbons for Meg.* (I)
33 Field, Elsie Kimmell. *Prairie Winter.* (P)
35 Garland, Hamlin. *Main-Travelled Roads.* (S)
36 Goble, Paul and Dorothy. *Lone Bull's Horse Raid.* (I)
40 Hays, Wilma Pitchford. *Little Yellow Fur.* (P)
51 Hueston, Ethel. *Calamity Jane of Deadwood Gulch.* (S)
52 ———— *Star of the West: The Romance of the Lewis and Clark Expedition.* (S)
59 Lane, Rose Wilder. *Free Land.* (S)
60 ———— *Let the Hurricane Roar.* (J, S)
64 Lenski, Lois. *Prairie School.* (I)
65 McNeely, Marian Hurd. *The Jumping-Off Place.* (I, J)
66 Manfred, Frederick. *The Golden Bowl.* (S)
67 Meigs, Cornelia. *The Willow Whistle.* (I)
70 Neihardt, John G. *When the Tree Flowered.* (S)
79 Rolvaag, Ole Edvart. *Giants in the Earth: A Saga of the Prairie.* (S)
80 Rounds, Glen. *The Blind Colt.* (I)
81 Sandoz, Mari. *The Horsecatcher.* (J, S)
86 Seibert, Jerry. *Sacajawea: Guide to Lewis and Clark.* (I)
87 Sneve, Virginia Driving Hawk. *Betrayed.* (J)
88 ———— *High Elk's Treasure.* (I)
93 Taylor, Don Alonzo. *Old Sam, Thoroughbred Trotter.* (I)
99 Veglahn, Nancy. *Follow the Golden Goose.* (I, J)
101 Wilder, Laura Ingalls. *By the Shores of Silver Lake.* (I, J, S)
102 ———— *The First Four Years.* (I, J, S)
104 ———— *Little Town on the Prairie.* (I, J, S)
105 ———— *The Long Winter.* (I, J, S)
106 ———— *These Happy Golden Years.* (I, J, S)

FOLKTALES

116 Botkin, Benjamin A., ed. *A Treasury of Western Folklore.* (S)
117 Dolch, Edward W., and Marguerite P. *Tepee Stories in Basic Vocabulary.* (P, I)
118 Federal Writers' Project, South Dakota. *Legends of the Mighty Sioux.* (I)

POETRY, DRAMA, MUSIC

125 Clark, Badger. *Sun and Saddle Leather: A Collection of Poems.* (I, J, S)

129 Garson, Eugenia, comp. *Laura Ingalls Wilder Songbook: Favorite Songs from the "Little House" Books.* (I, J, S)

132 Milton, John R., ed. *The Literature of South Dakota.* (S)

133 Neihardt, John G. *A Cycle of the West.* 5 vols. (S)

BIOGRAPHY AND PERSONAL ACCOUNTS

137 Anderson, Lavere. *Sitting Bull: Great Sioux Chief.* (P,I)

140 Black Elk, Oglala Indian. *Black Elk Speaks; Being the Life Story of a Holy Man of the Oglala Sioux, as told to John G. Neihardt (Flaming Rainbow).* (S)

151 Dines, Glen. *Crazy Horse.* (P)

155 Farnsworth, Frances Joyce. *Winged Moccasins: The Story of Sacajawea.* (J)

156 Felton, Harold W. *Nat Love, Negro Cowboy.* (I)

157 Fielder, Mildred. *Wild Bill and Deadwood.* (S)

161 Garland, Hamlin. *A Son of the Middle Border.* (S)

162 Garst, Shannon. *Crazy Horse, Great Warrior of the Sioux.* (I, J)

163 _____ *Sitting Bull: Champion of His People.* (J)

164 Garst, Shannon and Warren. *Wild Bill Hickok.* (J, S)

171 Haverstock, Mary Sayre. *Indian Gallery: The Story of George Catlin.* (J, S)

174 Holbrook, Stewart H. *Wild Bill Hickok Tames the West.* (I)

179 Johnson, Dorothy M. *Warrior for a Lost Nation: A Biography of Sitting Bull.* (I, J)

181 Jones, Gene. *Where the Wind Blew Free: Tales of Young Westerners.* (J, S)

183 Karolevitz, Robert F. *Where Your Heart Is: The Story of Harvey Dunn, Artist.* (S)

193 Meadowcroft, Enid LaMonte. *Crazy Horse: Sioux Warrior.* (P)

194 _____ *The Story of Crazy Horse.* (P, I)

203 O'Connor, Richard. *Sitting Bull: War Chief of the Sioux.* (I, J)

205 Plate, Robert. *Palette and Tomahawk: The Story of George Catlin July 27, 1796–December 23, 1872.* (J, S)

207 Rockwell, Anne. *Paintbrush & Peacepipe: The Story of George Catlin.* (I)

211 Sandoz, Mari. *Crazy Horse: The Strange Man of the Oglalas.* (S)

225 Van Nuys, Laura Bower. *The Family Band: From the Missouri to the Black Hills 1881–1900.* (S)

226 Veglahn, Nancy. *The Buffalo King: The Story of Scotty Philip.* (J)

228 Voight, Virginia Frances. *Sacajawea.* (P)

232 Wilder, Laura Ingalls. *On the Way Home: The Diary of a Trip from South Dakota to Mansfield, Missouri in 1894.* (J, S)

234 Wyman, Walker D. *Frontier Woman: The Life of a Woman Homesteader on the Dakota Frontier.* (S)

236 Zochert, Donald. *Laura: The Life of Laura Ingalls Wilder.* (J, S)

OTHER INFORMATIONAL BOOKS

243 Bailey, Bernadine. *Picture Book of South Dakota.* (I)

245 Beine, George Holmes. *Land of the Coyote.* (S)

246 Bennett, Estelline. *Old Deadwood Days.* (S)

247 Bjorklund, Lorence F. *Faces of the Frontier.* (I, J)

248 Blasingame, Ike. *Dakota Cowboy: My Life in the Old Days.* (S)

249 Bleeker, Sonia. *The Sioux Indians: Hunters and Warriors of the Plains.* (I, J)

253 *Brevet's South Dakota Historical Markers.* (S)

255 Burns, Paul C., and Hines, Ruth. *To Be a Pioneer.* (I)

256 Caras, Roger A. *The Custer Wolf: Biography of an American Renegade.* (S)

259 Casey, Robert J. *The Black Hills and Their Incredible Characters: A Chronicle and a Guide.* (S)

260 Clark, Champ. *The Badlands.* (J, S)

277 Gilfillan, Archer B. *Sheep: Life on the South Dakota Range.* (S)

294 Jennewein, J. Leonard, and Boorman, Jane, eds. *Dakota Panorama.* (S)

295 Jones, Evan, and the Editors of Time-Life Books. *The Plains States: Iowa, Kansas, Minnesota, Missouri, Nebraska, North Dakota, South Dakota.* (S)

296 Karolevitz, Robert F. *Challenge: The South Dakota Story.* (J, S)

299 Kohl, Edith Eudora. *Land of the Burnt Thigh.* (S)

302 Lauber, Patricia. *Dust Bowl: The Story of Man on the Great Plains.* (I, J)

303 Lewis, Faye Cashatt. *Nothing to Make a Shadow.* (S)

307 McCracken, Harold. *The American Cowboy.* (S)

311 Marriott, Alice. *Indians on Horseback.* (I, J)

322 Neihardt, John G. *The River and I.* (S)
325 Neuberger, Richard L. *The Lewis and Clark Expedition.* (I)
330 Oyan, Ethel R. *South Dakota for Young People.* (I)
336 Rounds, Glen. *Buffalo Harvest.* (I)
337 _____ *The Cowboy Trade.* (I)
339 _____ *The Treeless Plains.* (I)
343 Sandoz, Mari. *These Were the Sioux.* (J, S)
344 Schell, Herbert S. *History of South Dakota.* (S)
347 Standing Bear, Luther. *My People the Sioux.* (S)
350 Tallent, Annie D. *The Black Hills; or, The Last Hunting Grounds of the Dakotahs.* (S)
355 Veglahn, Nancy. *Getting to Know the Missouri River.* (I)
356 _____ *South Dakota.* (J)
357 Vestal, Stanley. *The Missouri.* (S)
367 Wyman, Walker D. *Nothing but Prairie and Sky: Life on the Dakota Range in the Early Days.* (S)

DIRECTORY OF REGIONAL PUBLISHERS
AND LOCAL BOOK SOURCES

The names and addresses of regional publishers not listed in *Books in Print* and of local book sources are provided as acquisitions aids.

Analytical Statistics
  Fargo, ND 58102

Arbor Printing Co.
  416 S. 11th
  Lincoln, NE 68508

Augstums Print Service
  1621 S. 17th
  Lincoln, NE 68502

Bethany College
  Lindsborg, KS 67456

Bismarck Tribune
  Box 1498
  222 Forth St.
  Bismarck, ND 58501

Cass County Historical Society
  West Fargo, ND 58102

Colby Community College
  1255 S. Range
  Colby, KS 67701

Educational Marketing
  and Research
  La Jolla, CA 92037

Kansas State Reading Circle
  715 W. 10th St.
  Topeka, KS 66612
  (source for some out-of-print and other Kansas materials)

Marion Piper
Box 98
Mohall, ND 58761

Nebraska Curriculum
Development Center
338 Andrews Hall
Lincoln, NE 68558

Northern School Supply Co.
NP Avenue and 8th St.
Fargo, ND 58102
(source for most North Dakota
regional publications)

Purcell's Inc.
Broken Bow, NE 68822

Salt Valley Press
427 Sharp Bldg.
Lincoln, NE 68508

Sierra Printing and Publishing Co.
2900 Rio Linda Blvd.
Sacramento, CA 95815

Sod House Society
221 S. 21 St.
Ord, NE 68862

Tri-College Center for
Environmental Studies
North Dakota State University
Fargo, ND 58102

The Westerner's Foundation
University of the Pacific
3601 Pacific Ave.
Stockton, CA 95204

AUTHOR-TITLE-
SUBJECT INDEX

Authors, subjects, and titles are included in one alphabetical list. Author entries appear in lightface type, subject entries in boldface type, and title entries in italic type. Each entry is followed by at least one boldface number which refers to the entry number assigned to every book listed in the Annotated Bibliography. For a subject entry of a work of fiction, only the entry number of the book is given. For a nonfiction subject entry, the book's entry number is all that is given if the entire book deals with the subject indicated. When only a specific section of the nonfiction book deals with the subject indicated, a colon follows the boldface entry number and the page number or numbers are added in lightface type. When an entry includes more than one reference, a semicolon separates the references. The symbol "SR" following a reference indicates additional references to the subject are scattered throughout the book.

Series design by Vladimir Reichl
Composed by FM Typesetting Company in Linotype
Times Roman with Futura Light display faces
Printed on 50# Warren's Olde Style, a pH neutral stock, and
bound by the University of Chicago Printing Department